Schools on Probation

D0555365

Schools on Probation

HOW ACCOUNTABILITY WORKS
(AND DOESN'T WORK)

Heinrich Mintrop

Teachers College, Columbia University
New York and London

Published by Teachers College Press, 1234 Amsterdam Avenue, New York, NY 10027

Library of Congress Cataloging-in-Publication Data

Mintrop, Heinrich.
    Schools on probation : how accountability works (and doesn't work) / Heinrich Mintrop.
        p. cm.
    Includes bibliographical references and index.
    ISBN 0-8077-4409-3 (pbk. : alk. paper) — ISBN 0-8077-4410-7 (cloth : alk. paper)
    1. Educational accountability—Maryland—Case studies.   2. Educational accountability—Kentucky—Case studies.   3. School improvement programs—Maryland—Case studies.   4. School improvement programs—Kentucky—Case studies.   I. Title.

    LB2806.22.M56 2004
    379.1'58'0973—dc21   2003054193

ISBN 0-8077-4409-3 (paper)
ISBN 0-8077-4410-7 (cloth)

Printed on acid-free paper
Manufactured in the United States of America

11 10 09 08 07 06 05 04   8 7 6 5 4 3 2 1

Contents

Acknowledgments

A NUMBER OF PEOPLE PARTICIPATED in the research project on which this book is based, and I would like to thank them here. Foremost are research assistants Daria Buese, Kim Curtis, Masako Nishio, and Margaret Fee Quintero as well as research associate Lea Plut-Pregelj. They contributed directly to various book chapters or sections therein. I want to thank Bob Pettit for his case study of a Kentucky school and Betty King for her invaluable field work in the Maryland schools. Ann MacLellan helped with her expertise in the content analysis of school improvement plans. I want to thank James Cibulka and Jane Clark Lindle for their support as co-principal investigators in the project. Jennifer O'Day was part of the early conceptualization of the research. Last but not least, I want to thank my partner James Romeo Holloway, who helped me with his cheers, encouragement, and tenacity. This study was supported by a grant from the Office of Educational Research and Improvement at the U.S. Department of Education. The views expressed in this book are those of the author alone.

Introduction

FAILING PUBLIC SCHOOLS are a national problem. Highly publicized reports and manifestos (Goals 2000, 1994; National Commission on Excellence in Education, 1983) have repeatedly put the spotlight on performance deficits in American schools. In recent years, more and more states and local districts have responded by creating standards-based accountability systems in the hope that such systems will provide incentives for educators to improve their performance. Policymakers and the public are eager to see the results. While high-stakes accountability systems have been proliferating in many states as a means to effect a productivity boost in schools statewide, they are particularly popular in urban systems as a means of addressing the highly publicized issue of failing urban schools. A new "no excuses" era of school reform has dawned, according to Hugh Price (1997), president of the Urban League: "There are no longer any excuses for the failure of inner-city students to achieve. The landscape of urban public education is dotted with teachers, classrooms, and even entire schools that deliver the goods" (p. 1). Educators are urged to avail themselves of new effective practices, and high-stakes accountability systems are designed to intensify the momentum for such willingness.

High-stakes school accountability is a bipartisan project. On the federal level, both Democrats and Republicans have pursued it. In his Fourth Annual State of American Education Address in 1997, then–U.S. Secretary of Education Richard Riley (1997) urged, "We need to stop making excuses and get on with the business of fixing our schools. If a school is bad and can't be changed, reconstitute it or close it down." In 2002, high-stakes accountability measures had become a cornerstone of President Bush's educational agenda. Redesigns of Title I legislation give ample consideration to testing and sanctions. Federal legislation signed by the president in 2002, the No Child Left Behind Act of 2001, has dramatically expanded the reach of high-stakes accountability in schools.

The section on Kentucky is based on a contribution by Margaret Quintero, research assistant in the study.

But many state governments acted prior to federal legislation. As of 2001, almost all 50 states had a testing program in place, 49 states had statewide academic standards, and 27 states had school accountability systems that identify low-performing schools. Fourteen states stipulated more severe penalties when an underperforming school fails to improve (Boser, 2001). However, only nine states financed student remediation and only seven states provided remedial funding to low-performing schools, according to the ratings of Quality Counts, a project of *Education Week* ("Quality Counts 2001," 2001).

In 1997 the city of Chicago alone identified a hundred or so public schools on probation that had fewer than 15% of their students reading at the national norm, as measured by the Iowa Test of Basic Skills (Chicago Public Schools, 1997). Between 1995 and 2001, the small state of Maryland identified a hundred or so schools statewide as low performing. Between 1999 and 2001 alone, the large state of California identified 1,290 persistently low-performing schools that are enrolled in the state's Immediate Intervention/ Underperforming Schools Program. Implementation of the new federal Title I legislation has added further impetus to the identification of thousands more low-performing schools across the country (Schemo, 2002).

What is more, these schools are not randomly or evenly distributed across the states; in many instances they are clustered in districts that have traditionally served poor and disadvantaged minority populations. For example, in Maryland, almost all identified schools are located in two districts; in California, 54 of the 1,000 or so school districts with more than 10 schools have had at least a third of their schools eligible for California's Immediate Intervention/ Underperforming Schools Program.

Thus, the proliferation of high-stakes accountability systems in the United States has fast created a new category of schools identified with various labels: schools on probation, schools under reconstitution, schools in decline or in crisis, schools under review, immediate intervention schools, schools eligible for assistance, and so on. In the public debate, these schools are also known summarily as *failing*. Each accountability system has created its own nomenclature, but the underlying gestalt is the same: Based on a small set of numerical performance indicators, accountability systems identify putative underperformers that are given a limited period of time to reverse growth deficits or decline and that are threatened with more severe penalties upon failure to do so. Performance indices and quantitative growth targets are calculated, often with intricate statistical algorithms, that communicate to educators that the status quo is no longer acceptable. Rather, continuous test score improvement in lower-performing schools is expected, often at higher rates than in top-performing schools. For schools that fail to live up to these new expectations, sanctions such as probation, reconstitution, loss of accreditation, state takeover, zero-based staffing, and the like have been added to the educational policy arsenal.

Yet, despite the growing popularity of "get tough" measures across the United States, there is scant evidence of the policies' benefits. In most states and districts the imposition of sanctions on low-performing schools is still nascent. In a few, among them the states of Maryland and Kentucky, high-stakes accountability measures have been in place since the early 1990s and experiences have accumulated, but systematic studies of schools that labor under sanctions are sparse. But policymaking does not move at the speed of research. It moves more slowly when research suggests solutions that go against the grain of public sentiment and more swiftly when, according to the spirit of the times, a policy measure makes intuitive sense as a sorely needed solution to an intractable problem that policymakers feel compelled to address.

As states increasingly identify schools with performance deficits and as the numbers of schools that operate under various sanctions and penalties proliferate, our knowledge gap becomes acutely felt. Knowledge about the effect of "get tough" policies is imperative for another reason. Not only are the benefits of these policies not systematically documented, but the potential costs of sanctions call for careful scrutiny. High-stakes measures can be contentious and divisive, if events in San Francisco (Ruenzel, 1997) or Philadelphia (Johnston, 2000; Jones, 1997) are any indication. They can pit state, local districts, unions, schools, administrators, and teachers against one another and upset the kind of consensus among policymakers, administrators, and teachers that scholars of earlier stages of school reform deemed essential for success (Elmore, 1990).

HOW SANCTIONS MIGHT WORK

Policies intended to induce changes in policy recipients' behavior are designed with a specific theory of failure and a theory of action in mind. They make (often implicit) assumptions about their target problem and anticipate a way in which policy recipients will change their behavior. Redistributive policies (Peterson, Rabe, & Wong, 1991), for example, are guided by the assumption that low performance of schools is substantively a result of underresourced learning environments. A high frequency of low-performing students in particular schools would be evidence of the schools' need for additional resources. Incentive policies, on the other hand, place the burden of responsibility for poor performance on employees' work effort. Underperformance becomes associated with failing teachers and administrators. Incentive policies centrally target will rather than capacity or resources (Thompson & Zeuli, 1999).

High-stakes policies bank on the motivational power of sanctions, currently conceptualized in two ways. In one version, popular among economists concerned about the spiraling cost of education, high-stakes accountability is resource-neutral. Improvements occur as a result of changed orientations and dispositions toward work effort (Hanushek, 1994). In another version, strongly advocated by researchers around the Consortium for Policy Research in Education (CPRE), sanctions, such as probation or reconstitution, attain their motivational power in conjunction with new resources needed for capacity building in schools that fail as much for lack of will as for insufficient capacity (Fuhrman & Elmore, 2001; O'Day, Goertz, & Floden, 1995; O'Day & Smith, 1993). Thus, in the first version, clear performance goals, incentives, and sanctions make new resources unnecessary, while in the second version they make new resources more effective. But in either case, the motivational power of incentives and sanctions on individuals or organizations is assumed or implied.

In fact, we could probably dispense with the whole superstructure of high stakes that many states have built up in the last few years and return to more traditional redistributive grant-making patterns if it were not for the belief in the power of incentives and sanctions to improve low-performing or failing schools. The power of incentives and sanctions is even more crucial in state systems that place the accountability burden on schools rather than districts. In such systems, incentives and sanctions must compensate for the states' limited capacity to directly regulate or administer remote school actors.

Generally speaking, while there is some research on the effect of high-stakes accountability on schools generally (Firestone, Mayrowetz, & Fairman, 1998; Firestone & Pennel, 1993; Fuhrman & Odden, 2001; Kelley, 1999; Kelley, Conley, & Kimball, 2000; Kelley & Protsik, 1997; McNeil, 2000; Newmann, King, & Rigdon, 1997; Stecher, Barron, Chun, & Ross, 2000; Whitford, 2000), little research on the role of sanctions in low-performing schools is available (Brady, 2003; Gray, 2000; Hess, 1999a, 1999b; Malen, Croninger, Muncey, & Redmond-Jones, 2002; Mintrop, 2003; O'Day, 2003; Stoll & Meyers, 1998; Wong, Anagnostopoulos, & Rutledge, 1998; Wong, Anagnostopoulos, Rutledge, Lynn, & Dreeben, 1999) despite the proliferation of the phenomenon. But the absence of research does not necessarily mean that "little or nothing is established" (Wilcox & Gray, 1996, p. 3) or, as researchers would have it, that nothing "is known." While perhaps holding little appeal to the education profession that is subjected to it, probation and sanctions must make intuitive sense for those who decree and design accountability systems.

Although we have never seen policymakers and designers of accountability systems explicitly spell out why the labeling of schools as low-performing and the threat of further penalties would be effective motivators in educational settings, one could imagine the following intuitive scenario unfolding on the levels of individual teacher motivation, organizational development, and instructional change:

1. High-stakes accountability improves teacher motivation. When a school is publicly labeled as deficient, teachers, after going through a whole range of emotions, accept the urgency of improvement. This urgency is reinforced by the discomfort caused by state audits and the like. Teachers and administrators want to repair their public image, but they also take responsibility for the quality of their work. So, they take a critical look at their own work and reflect on the valid performance demands of the accountability system. They finally decide to increase effort in their own classrooms and get involved in the improvement of their school. Teachers who are highly committed to their school are especially motivated. Additional support that might accompany probation is appreciated and put to good use, but fresh resources are not essential for increasing one's effort in the classroom.

2. High-stakes accountability positively affects organizational development. Most accountability systems hold whole schools, rather than individuals, accountable for higher performance, and it is therefore through school-wide improvement that individuals overcome the label of probation. The label of probation throws the school into crisis but at the same time makes people realize that "we are in this together." Intense dialogue, perhaps even conflict, around the discrepancy between the current situation of the school and the state's performance demands ensues. Eventually the faculty pulls together around a set of shared expectations that are the basis for a formal structure of internal accountability. Test data and other indictors bring shortcomings into focus. All parts of the school are evaluated. Planning and more vigilant monitoring make the school more effective, and with determined leadership the school learns new strategies to turn itself around.

3. The eventual result is instructional change in classrooms. Given the ambitious performance-based character of the accountability systems studied here, schools, in order to master probation successfully, need to compel students not only to work harder but also to learn differently. Higher work intensity, tighter lesson plans, but also higher-order thinking and teamwork become paramount. When teachers have the will to change and faculties have begun to evaluate the shortcomings of their school, raise their own expectations to the high demands of the system, and agree on formal procedures of internal accountability, the conditions are ripe for a restructuring of teaching content and methods. Under these circumstances, probation will have worked.

THE TWO STATES

The data on which this book is based were collected in two states, Maryland and Kentucky. In recent years, these two states have garnered national acclaim ("Quality Counts 2001," 2001) for centering their accountability systems on tests that went beyond basic literacy and numeracy by asking students to perform complex learning operations, experiments, cooperative projects, complex essays, and portfolios. Although both states have by now simplified the complex tests with which they started out, our data were collected at a time when these tests were still in use, although, as in the case of Kentucky, already contested. Thus, in studying probation in the Maryland and Kentucky contexts, we are able to see what educators think and do within pedagogically complex accountability systems that are attuned to ambitious subject-matter standards.

Naturally, there is more to an accountability system than student learning assessments. There are nonacademic performance indicators (such as attendance), rewards and sanctions, selection criteria for low-performing schools, exit criteria for probation, school governance requirements, planning mandates, monitoring systems, and supports for building capacity at schools. These elements are embedded in authority relationships among schools, districts, and the state. And they are often in flux as political coalitions shift and new plans are advanced by state policymakers (Cibulka & Lindle, 2001), making accountability systems truly moving targets of study.

At the time the study was conducted between 1997 and 2000, both states had features of elaborate accountability systems in common: complex student assessments, performance categories for schools, rewards and sanctions, school improvement planning and monitoring. "Naming and shaming," threatening more severe penalties, and signaling public urgency and support were major mechanisms of probation meant to impel individual educators and schools to improve. But within this basic structure, the systems differed in some respects. Compared to Maryland, the Kentucky reform was more comprehensive, more rule-bound and scripted, but also more contested and in transition (Pankratz & Petrosko, 2000). The Maryland accountability system was more radical in its performance demands and also more consensual at the time. With regard to low-performing schools, Kentucky targeted growth deficits on all performance levels while Maryland identified only rock-bottom performers as probationary.

Maryland

The Maryland school accountability system, in place since 1993, had been fairly stable until recently. The state created its own performance-based test

(MSPAP, Maryland State Performance Assessment Program), which it administered in all elementary and middle schools, but beyond the assessments the state provided little instructional guidance. The MSPAP was given overwhelming weight in a school performance index (SPI) that was calculated for each school. Attendance rates and the Maryland Functional Tests (MFT), given in middle schools, had lesser weight. The MFTs were basic skills tests in a standardized multiple-choice format. The MSPAP was given in grades 3, 5, and 8 in reading, writing, language usage, mathematics, science, and social studies to measure student performance on tasks requiring critical thinking, problem solving, and the integration of knowledge from multiple fields of study. Some notable features of the test were randomly selected groups of students who performed complex performance tasks and written explanations of problem-solving processes that were scored with rubrics. The state established a variety of performance targets that challenged some of the best schools in the state. In elementary and middle schools, acceptable measures were a 94% attendance rate and the attainment of a 70% satisfactory performance rate on the MSPAP.

The Maryland State Department of Education (MSDE) used the SPI to determine which schools would be subject to state intervention. The state created the status of probation, or "reconstitution eligibility," later renamed "local reconstituting," and the status of actual reconstitution, which was equivalent to state takeover. Reconstitution-eligible schools characteristically performed far below the standard and had declined from previous performance levels (Maryland State Department of Education, 1997). The number of schools designated as reconstitution-eligible by the state was limited by the MSDE's capacity to provide assistance to low-performing schools. The state superintendent retained much discretion in the identification process, and the state did not necessarily put every school that was eligible for reconstitution on probationary status.

Schools placed on probation were required to submit a school improvement plan to the state superintendent. The school improvement plan was to be written according to a template developed by the MSDE. The plan included school history and demographics, declared school mission, priorities and goals, as well as specific steps to improve the school program, proposed technical support, and professional development. A budget also had to be submitted indicating how money would be allocated to provide for the indicated improvements. The plan was subject to approval by the state board of education. The state provided small school improvement grants for reconstitution-eligible schools, but it was up to local districts to decide on the manner of disbursement. These grants could be used only for professional development and curricular improvements. Of the two districts studied here, one allocated these funds directly to schools; the other also did so in the earlier years of the program's existence but subsequently folded these funds into the larger special-needs budget. Schools that participated in the study received earmarked reconstitution funds between $0 and $150,000 yearly.

State auditing teams and state monitors visited identified schools to help in the diagnosis of needs and oversee implementation of the plan. The state monitors were the "eyes and ears" of the state; they did not fulfill the role of change agents in schools. Although often experienced educators or retired administrators, they had not received extensive training for their role, nor did they have the time to get intensely involved in individual schools.

Up to the 1999–2000 schoolyear, the state had put 98 schools on probation, five-sixths of them located in the state's largest city, which eventually had about half of its schools identified. Poverty levels and ethnic minority populations in the schools were very high. For example, a median 77% for the 82 elementary and middle schools identified up until 1998 participated in the federal program for free or reduced-price lunches. Over 80% of enrolled students were African American.

MSPAP test score data over time show that identified schools posted only modest performance increments and developed unevenly, but they did keep up with the rest of the state and other high-poverty schools in the state. At least initially, schools with a record of low performance and marked deterioration reversed the worst declines, but the effect was not lasting or consistent.

Marginal positive effects notwithstanding, it is apparent that, up to 2000, probation did not spur performance increases for the majority of schools on the scale needed to swiftly lessen their tremendous performance lag. Instead, large gaps persisted. In 2000, the mean percentage of students passing the MSPAP with satisfactory performance or better for the 1996 cohort of reconstitution-eligible schools was 16% in fifth-grade reading and 9% in eighth-grade reading, a far cry from the state's anticipated 70% rate.*

Up until 2000, three schools successfully exited the system. Final sanctions were applied to three others. These three were taken over by the state and contracted to a private school management firm. Reconstitution-eligibility (RE) in Maryland, rather than a transitory stage, appeared to be a protracted period of probation for schools facing exceptionally arduous challenges. Thus, we need to explain why schools seem to improve somewhat, but also why change is not more dramatic.

For the case studies on which this book is based, we selected seven schools from the two districts most impacted by probation—three elementary schools

---

*See the Technical Report (Part 2) of the study for more detailed statistical analysis. Available online at: www.gseis.ucla.edu/faculty/mintrop

and four middle schools. These schools were visited over a period of 2 to 3 years from 1998 to 2000. Five schools were new to the program in 1998 while two of them had been put on probation in 1994. (For more details on the case selection, please consult the Appendix.)

Kentucky

In 1990, the Kentucky General Assembly passed HB 940, the Kentucky Education Reform Act (KERA), in response to a 1989 State Supreme Court decision that declared the commonwealth's system of public schooling to be unconstitutional due to the inequity and inadequacy of funding provided for schools. KERA created accountability standards for all students, provided curriculum content guidelines, and mandated assessments that reflected these standards. KERA also required that schools be governed by a site-based decision-making (SBDM) council representative of parents, teachers, and administrators.

In time, the state developed a rather detailed core curriculum that guided instruction and circumscribed the content of the assessments—the Kentucky Instructional Results Information System (KIRIS), later redesigned and re-named Commonwealth Accountability Testing System (CATS). The original tests included student responses on open-ended and multiple-choice questions in reading, math, science, social studies, art/humanities, and practical living/vocational courses, as well as scores on student writing portfolios. These academic components—combined with nonacademic measures of attendance, retention, dropout rates and the successful transition to adult life—resulted in a composite index score for each school. Based on this score, the Kentucky Department of Education (KDE) set a school-specific baseline index and biennial school-specific growth targets. This was the level of achievement for which the school was held accountable. The system impelled schools to strive for continuous improvement of their scores. All schools were to reach the same achievement level after a period of about 20 years regardless of initial baseline performance (by now extended to 2014). Schools surpassing their predetermined index were eligible for rewards, while schools falling below the mark were eligible for state assistance in efforts to improve the school. Since CATS, schools are also compared to a band of other schools performing on the same level. In the Kentucky system, schools on all performance levels could enter probation, though schools with the lowest baseline scores had the largest gains to make each biennium.

At the time of the study, Kentucky had two basic categories of low-performing schools. If a school scored below its last biennium scores by not more than 5%, it was declared "in decline." If a school scored significantly below its accountability baseline (5% or more below its previous biennium scores), it was declared "in crisis." Schools that were in decline for two consecutive biennia could also enter the "in crisis" stage. Schools designated as "in decline" were required to participate in the School Transformation and Renewal Program (STAR). Once in the program, they were required to write a school transformation plan and were assigned a sort of probation manager to assist in the implementation of the transformation plan. Initially, intervention in schools not performing at expected levels was mandatory. However, since 1998 schools "in-decline" could opt out of the state assistance program, but they were still required to write and submit a plan.

As part of STAR, Kentucky created the role of the distinguished educator (DE), later renamed the highly skilled educator (HSE). DEs or HSEs were teachers or administrators who worked with schools to improve their curriculum and instruction and to implement the school improvement plan (David, Kannapel, & McDiarmid, 2000). The HSEs led schools through the planning process by assisting in the collection and analysis of data, identification of causes of decline, and provision of feedback about goals and suggestions of possible strategies for reaching these goals.

Once a school was declared "in crisis," sanctions and penalties were to intensify. The school had to notify parents of the right to transfer their children to a more successful school. By design, what happened to a school was then in the hands of the DE/HSEs. They had the authority to make all decisions previously made by staff, assist in curriculum practices, promote community engagement, and coordinate external reviews. The DE/HSEs could evaluate all staff members every 6 months in accordance with standards developed in teachers' individual growth plans. At the end of the evaluation period, DE/HSEs could recommend the dismissal or transfer of any school staff member who failed to meet the growth goal or was judged to be acting in a manner resistant to improvement efforts. All such disciplinary actions were dealt with on an individual basis. Although the envisioned final sanctions were severe, they were never fully applied. In schools designated "in decline," the DE/HSE's role was more advisory.

In order to graduate from STAR, schools had to meet the original threshold goal that had put them into the STAR program. Because the state changed the format of the test from KIRIS to CATS in the middle of our study, we could not carry out the kind of quantitative analysis that was possible for the Maryland schools. The only indications we have about the success of probation in Kentucky are entrance and exit statistics. From 1993 to 1996, the state entered 53 schools into the STAR program, of which 16 did not manage to exit probation. For the next biennium (1996–1998) an additional 250 schools were identified. Most of those schools did not continue in the status. But their exit coincided with a redesign of the system. Because of the change in tests, new baselines had to be established and no new schools were identified in 1998. Although the overwhelming majority of schools had successfully exited their probation as of 1998, the disruption of continuity in the accountability system makes interpretation of these figures difficult.

For the case studies on which this book is based, we selected four schools from Kentucky—two elementary and two middle schools. Two of the schools were repeaters in the program, while two were newly identified in 1998. To enhance comparability between the two states, three of the Kentucky schools were very low performers and, not unlike their counterparts in Maryland, exceptionally impacted by poverty and serving above-average proportions of ethnic minority students. (Consult the Appendix for further details on case selection and data collection.)

ORGANIZATION OF THE BOOK

This book contributes to filling the knowledge gap about high-stakes accountability in low-performing schools. It describes what schools do when they are put on probation, that is, when state governments use the public stigma of low performance and the prospect of more severe penalties to challenge educators to improve their schools. The book concentrates on difficult schools, those traditionally serving students from poor and disadvantaged minority background. We wanted to know how probation in low-performing schools of this character influences teachers' motivation and behavior: Does it spell defeat or is it a call to action? Does it raise job commitment or does it add impetus to exit? Does it rally highly professional teachers or does it put them off? Does it induce learning within school faculties or does it freeze them up? And lastly, does it help teachers make instructional changes or is its impact repelled at the classroom doors as with reform waves preceding it (Cuban, 1984)? And if it pushes through, how does this come about?

Thus the book examines schools' responses on three levels: individual teacher motivation, organizational development, and instructional change. These levels constitute the three main parts of the book. On each level we look at crucial issues that may be decisive for the impact of probation on school improvement. When we look at teacher motivation in Part I, we are of course interested in the intensity of the motivational stimulus of sanctions, but we also need to know in more detail exactly what motives are spurred by probation, because we assume that this will have important repercussions for the kinds of improvement processes that might get underway on the organizational and classroom levels.

Teachers, for example, may reject the low-performance label as unjustified pressure, they may respond to it out of concern for their own professional well-being, or they may be motivated to reflect critically about their work. Depending on these sentiments, they may embrace the challenge and commit to their school's improvement or flee the negative label. In Chapter 1, we examine the emotions and sentiments that are triggered by the new pressures of probation. In Chapter 2, we explore whether the accountability system is seen as a meaningful guide and occasion for reflection on teachers' work. In Chapter 3, we conclude our investigation of individual motivation by looking at various dispositions and contextual factors, systemic and up-close, that may explain teachers' willingness to become engaged, exert effort, and stay committed to their negatively labeled school.

In Part II, our emphasis shifts to the organizational level. We look at two key aspects, organizational interactions and strategies for programmatic improvement. We pay particular attention to what distinguishes schools that move and improve as a result of probation (Chapter 4) from those that get stuck in decline or stagnation (Chapter 5). In Chapter 6, we look beyond our focal case study schools by comparing them with patterns found in the Kentucky schools and with patterns found in a larger number of school improvement plans. Finally, we conclude the organization-level analysis with a discussion of administrative control versus organizational learning in schools on probation.

In Part III, we shift from the organizational level of the whole school to the classroom. We describe patterns of instructional change observed in the schools with the help of vignettes from teachers whom we visited in their classrooms (Chapter 7). We discuss the scope of teachers' instructional efforts given the pedagogical complexity of accountability demands and added pressures of probation.

In the Conclusion, we summarize how educators individually and organizationally cope with high-stakes accountability in their labeled low-performing schools and derive lessons from their behavior. We point to pitfalls that teachers and administrators ought to avoid and challenges they might want to embrace. Finally, we make suggestions for improvements in accountability system designs so that more educators may respond to high-stakes accountability in an educationally meaningful way.

Advocates of high-stakes accountability hope that the public exposure of low performance and the threat of further sanctions will move educators to increase work effort and schools to get organized and focused on student achievement. This book shows, in a nutshell, that probation had a weak motivational effect on most educators. The case is different for administrators and small groups of highly involved teachers. Teachers modestly strove to increase test scores and overcome probation primarily because of a desire to be rid of the negative label and diffuse commitment to their school, not because they expected a clear reward. Nor did they consider accountability goals as particularly meaningful orientations for their work. Those teachers who become more active were not necessarily also more committed to staying at their negatively labeled school. Many teacher activists responded to the challenge of probation, but at the same time wished to leave their schools.

What schools did under probation largely depended on how principals reacted to the low-performance status. In our sample of schools, proactive principals increased administrative control and relied on the know-how of instructional specialists to intensify test preparation, curricular alignment, and the implementation of new instructional materials and programs, often prescriptive and mandated by district administrations. In this way, high-stakes accountability or probation, originally conceptualized as a motivational tool for schools to focus and engage in active problem solving out of self-interest (Hanushek, 1994), increasingly became a managerial tool to prepare teachers in labeled schools to comply with externally chosen solutions for the schools' supposed failings.

Such compliance may be suitable for an accountability system centered on basic skills assessments of low pedagogical complexity, but is insufficient for the kind of ambitious instructional reform that the two states examined here set out to accomplish. But we argue that policymakers and school practitioners can learn from the patterns exhibited by the schools we studied—namely, how accountability designs need to be altered and how schools need to redirect their efforts to compensate for the "meaning deficit" and "control defaults" of high-stakes accountability for teachers.

PART I

Teacher Motivation and Probation

THE PRESSURES OF PROBATION—that is, the stigma of being labeled "low-performing"; the threat of further, perhaps more severe sanctions; and the experience of increased control that comes with new planning requirements, audits, and so on—may make teachers in low-performing schools more susceptible to external directions and provide incentives to focus on the goals of the state accountability system and put more emphasis on raising test scores.

But probation pressures may also cause anxiety and concern about professional reputation, perhaps leading to diminishing job satisfaction. Job satisfaction affects turnover and absenteeism (Ingersoll, 2001), and rather than compelling workers to exert effort and instilling the will to high performance, pressures from negative sanctions are sometimes avoided with exit (Vroom, 1964), particularly where exit options are abundant. Thus, the punitive nature of probation may result in diminished commitment to remain associated with the negatively impacted school. Research on burnout (Dworkin, 1987; Ingersoll, 2001; LeCompte & Dworkin, 1991) highlights this concern by identifying low morale and commitment as key problems besetting schools in the urban milieu. These problems are facilitated by school disorder, discipline problems, and controlling and unsupportive leadership.

On the other hand, satisfied workers are not necessarily the most motivated workers, and challenge, discomfort, and perhaps even stress may be potentially positive stimuli for increased work energy (Lawler, 1973). Rather, employees are motivated to exert effort when they face a task with challenging goals and attainable rewards that they feel competent to attain (Odden & Kelley, 1997; Rowan, Chiang, & Miller, 1997). If teachers see a connection between individual effort and expected rewards and have the requisite capacity to reach their goals, if they deem the attainment of the reward likely and the goal as realistic, and if they value the expected reward itself (e.g., consider high test scores or exit from probation as important), this motivational model predicts that teachers will improve their performance. Incentive systems, such as high-stakes accountability, are designed with such goal attainment and reward expectancy models (Lawler, 1973) in mind.

Teachers may act out of self-interest. In this case, the reward for their efforts would be the repair of their reputation, avoidance of more serious penalties, or a monetary incentive, if such is provided by the system. They may also act out of a sense of responsibility (Abelmann, Elmore, Even, Kenyon, & Marshall, 1999) for a standard of work quality. In this case, the judgments of the accountability system (i.e., the low-performance label) would be accepted as fair and valid assessments of one's teaching and probation would be more intrinsically motivating.

The importance of more intrinsic motives is stressed by those who doubt the applicability of reward and goal-setting models for schools. According to Shamir (1991), these models presuppose "strong situations" (p. 406) with clearly identifiable relationships among increased effort, performance, and reward. But in schools, rewards for teachers are less abundant; there is less tendency to differentiate among individuals on the basis of work performance because of collective orientations; and links among work effort, results, and rewards are more difficult to construct. In these situations, work motivation is better explained with a "diffuse and open-ended concept of commitment" (p. 408) to performance goals that become internalized and instill "meaning" into individuals as they "connect the individual to the concerns that transcend his own limited personal existence" (p. 409). Following these lines of thinking, teachers' work motivation is better explained by internal standards and internalized performance norms of the work group, rather than rational self-interest (Johnson, 1990). Personally meaningful standards are often diffuse, rather than enshrined in specific goals and receivable rewards.

High-stakes accountability systems introduce features into educators' workplaces, such as clear quantitative performance targets connected to performance statuses, that may make their work situation "stronger" and increase momentum for rational goal and reward maximizing (Kelley & Protsik, 1997), but the meaningfulness of the accountability system may nevertheless be crucial if one aims at critical self-reflection and the sustenance of commitment to a potentially negative work situation.

This is particularly true for group accountability under which the school as a whole is held accountable rather than teachers individually. Now success (goal or reward attainment) is tied not only to individual effort and competence but also to the energy and capacity of all organizational members (Hanushek, 1994; Malen, 1999; Mohrman, Mohrman, & Odden, 1996). Group accountability then seems to presuppose a degree of trust and more diffuse commitment to the work group. Particularly, highly motivated and highly performing teachers are in need of this commitment to offset dissatisfaction and exit tendencies (Darling-Hammond, 1997) stemming from the summary application of the probation label independently of individual effort and engagement.

These more theoretical considerations inform our inquiry in Part I. We first explore how individual teachers deal with the new pressures of probation (Chapter 1). We find out whether they are roused by them and accept them as well as whether they remain committed to their school despite these pressures. Then we widen the lens. We assume that probation is meaningful to teachers to the degree that they recognize the accountability system as valid, fair, and realistic. When teachers consider their accountability system as meaningful, they may be more likely to link the low-performance label with their own work (Chapter 2). In Chapter 3, we round out the picture. We construct a profile of the teacher most motivated by probation by illuminating the relationship among pressures, meanings, individual competence and organizational capacity on the one hand, and levels of work motivation and commitment on the other.

CHAPTER 1

The Pressure of Sanctions

NOT SO LONG AGO it would have been rather unusual for a state government to expose schools under its jurisdiction as failing. It would have been unusual for teachers as they watched the morning news or read the morning newspaper to hear or see their school's name mentioned in a lineup of failing schools. Although it was no secret then that some schools were better or worse than others, such knowledge was informal. Accountability systems add a new quality: Knowledge of low performance is now based on clear measures, is authoritative, and is in the public eye. The message is that the public expects action from educators.

Educators, for their part, go through a whole swirl of emotions and sentiments when confronted with the low-performance label. Distilled from our interview and survey material, we found that for many teachers in these schools probation comes as a shock at first, soon to be followed by distancing one's own culpability from the label. The label becomes reinterpreted as a sign of the school's need for help. Many teachers, by contrast, reassert their own competence in the face of the state's negative verdict and scornfully reject the punitiveness of probation. Only a relatively small minority sees the label as good pressure, as momentum for teachers to get their act together. For the majority, getting rid of the label is a matter of public reputation. In the following, we describe these varied reactions in more detail.

SHOCK AND DISTANCING

Probation, according to our survey, instilled anxiety in teachers:

> Oh, I was terrified at first. . . . Just something about it just terrified me. I said . . . "Well, maybe we're not doing our jobs well," you know. But I know our teachers are doing the best that they can . . . I felt like, that a lot of us were just going to get transferred or . . . I don't know. . . . I was very fearful. (F-6)*

---

*Throughout this book, interview codes consist of a marker for the interviewee's school and a unique number. A through G refer to the seven Maryland schools, and 10 through 40 refer to the four Kentucky schools.

On the survey, 42% of respondents felt more anxious about their careers despite the fact that up to the time of the survey neither state had carried out sanctions that negatively impacted teachers personally. Anxiety was more prevalent among Kentucky teachers. In the four Kentucky schools, more than half of all teachers felt more anxious.

Senior teachers took probation especially to heart as an embarrassment and assault on their professional self-worth and reputation, as the vivid accounts from some teachers illustrate:

> I took it very personally, because of the efforts that I've made in the years that I've been here. And I really took it personally. It was almost like I had broken an arm, and I was in a lot of pain that particular day, and I internalized it, because I spend a lot of time after hours here, spend a lot of time preparing for labs, and you know, cleaning up after labs. So, I really took it personally. (A-19; eighth-grade science teacher)

> [I was] very demoralized. I felt really down. I felt like everyone would think I was a failure and a bad teacher because I feel like that's where all of the accountability is. It's on the teachers. . . . It's in the paper every day: "_____ Middle School in Decline" and you read that, and when someone says, "Where do you work?" and you answer, they're like, "Oh, that's that school." That's very disheartening when you work as hard as you work as a teacher. (20-09; middle school language arts teacher)

> I was embarrassed by it . . . and [I had] a sense of almost helplessness. (B-7)

But this initial reaction of personalizing probation wore off and, in time, a process of distancing set in, with teachers finding ways to absolve themselves from culpability. Novice teachers, of whom they were many, reminded themselves that they could hardly be causing the problem because of their short tenure, like the teacher who recounted this dialogue among colleagues:

> There were some other teachers, I think, who were newer teachers who were like, "Oh . . . it's so bad, . . ." I'm like, we weren't here when it happened, so don't get upset by it. . . . I feel confident in myself, what I'm doing, and I feel as though as a teacher, I am doing what I'm supposed to do to make sure that the kids understand the lesson. (B-8)

Others came to realize that teachers were not the only ones who should be held responsible and that one teacher alone was not carrying the burden ["It's not just myself!" (C-9)]. Many felt relieved of responsibility by reassuring themselves of their own personal competence and worth as professional educators despite the negative label, like this elementary school principal:

> I viewed it as a very negative cast over the school and over me, because I thought it was basically speaking about my instructional leadership. But then, on reflection, I realized that it wasn't about me. I wasn't going to make it be about me personally, and if I were to, in any way, salvage the morale of the people with whom I was working, and also say to people outside of myself, because I'd already convinced myself that I'm quite capable and able to do the things that I set out to do. . . . So, once I, on reflection, cleared my head of any guilt feelings, then I was able to move forward. (E-7; elementary school principal)

REINTERPRETATION: PROBATION AS NEED FOR HELP

Despite their apprehensions about the low-performance label, most teachers could not imagine that the state would carry through with its threats to close schools and fire teachers. Some teachers thought that this would simply not be "practical" (20-11), since not too many qualified applicants were ready to take their jobs in the first place: "I don't perceive there being a line of people lined up for our jobs and so no, I don't fear it" (10-06). Others counted on the professional insights of top decision makers, who surely knew that performance did not depend on teachers alone. Thus, final sanctions were "unreal," particularly for Kentucky teachers, who potentially faced harsher sanctions than their Maryland colleagues:

> I don't know that it wouldn't happen, but it's hard to kind of see someone coming and closing down the whole school and saying, "You've all been in decline for so long. You are continually going down as far as those test scores." I guess it's just hard to imagine, but there is that kind of fear there that there could be position changes or people from outside coming in. (40-14; middle school creative writing teacher)

Teachers in Maryland also could not quite picture what final sanctions could look like. In one district, many knew of a few schools that the district had subjected to zero-based staffing with reportedly disastrous results (Finkelstein et al., 2000). "The schools truly didn't change. It was as if it was destined for the scores to drop no matter what" (B-1; District B). Consequently, they did not expect a repeat of that in the near future. For some, state takeover, the final sanction in Maryland, merely meant that "well, instead of [the district] telling us what to do, the state will" (E-9).

Reinterpreting the high-stakes stance of the accountability system in their favor, teachers in both states hoped that probation was not meant to be punitive. Particularly in Maryland's District B, where fewer schools were on probation, low-performance status was associated with more funds, personnel, and resources. In District A, hope for resources was more vague, but the certainty was stronger that not too much would happen as a result of probation. Therefore, for the principal of School A, probation was:

> a blessing in disguise, and I've communicated that to the staff, and they're actually following my lead. . . . So, they've promised us quite a bit of money and resources and if they deliver, . . . I think there will be quite a few things we'll be able to do; so, it doesn't bother me that we're reconstitution eligible. (A-1)

The reading specialist in the same school echoed a similar sentiment, which was bolstered by the way district and school administrators communicated the meaning of the new status to teachers. As a result, she, like many of her colleagues in other schools, associated probation with more help, and hope for help and confidence in one's own effort and ability assuaged fear and disappointment.

The dire need for resources experienced by many schools made teachers accept probation as a necessary evil. A teacher in a large inner-city middle school said:

> I've always worked at very poor schools, where we barely had [enough], and you know, we had to personally spend our own money to even do labs or whatever. So, I felt that, number one, being reconstituted there would be available resources that I wasn't normally accustomed to. . . . I didn't see it as a threat. (D-2)

When teachers interpreted the low-performance status in the tradition of redistributive policies—that is, when they saw probation as an indication of need for fresh support and new resources rather than as a sign of failure to perform—they wondered what was the point of the punitive label. For them, "the stigma is the minus, but the programs that come about from that are a plus." One middle school teacher, weighing the positive against the negative, concluded about probation: "I think it's good, but I think that they should get rid of the bad stigma that goes with it" (B-5; District B). In Kentucky, teachers associated probation or "in decline" status with the services of a distinguished or highly skilled educator (DE/HSE). "Obviously we wished that it . . . was not necessary, but I'm glad that we have the help of someone [the HSE] to try and meet the needs of the children" (10-06).

Many teachers in both states bemoaned that "to get the help that you've been asking for, something negative has to happen." It would actually have to take such a punitive label for the state and the districts to come forward with additional support and attention. "You can't just ask for the help when you need it" (A-2; eighth-grade science teacher). Thus, probation became a mixed signal and overcoming probation a dilemma, as the principal of School C in an informal conversation noted: On the one hand, he wanted to be rid of the stigma through continuous improvement of the test scores, but on the other hand, he did not feel he could afford to lose the probation label altogether.

REASSERTION OF COMPETENCE

Teachers in the 11 schools on probation had a high sense of competence. On the survey, large majorities of teachers gave themselves the highest ratings on subjective indicators of professional competence and quality. Between two-thirds and three-fourths saw themselves as well prepared and highly effective and caring, with a strong sense of efficacy, with skills that matched the challenge of accountability and high performance, and with the willingness to exert above-average effort.

Indeed, all Kentucky teachers in the sample possessed at least a B.A., 71% reported having at least an M.A., and only 7% were reportedly not certified or not fully certified for the field they taught. But the figures for the Maryland sample were lower: 5% had not completed a B.A., and about one-third were uncertified or not fully certified for the field they taught. Most of the respondents who were not fully certified (73%) were within their first 3 years of teaching.

Tenure at school sites was biased toward the shorter term, with 53% of responding teachers in Kentucky and 71% in Maryland having been at their schools for 5 years or less. In the Maryland sample, almost one-half of respondents (46%) had been teaching for 5 years or less. In two Maryland schools, the average number of years at the current school was just 3 years. Presumably the Maryland schools on probation, more so than the Kentucky schools, were adversely affected by the mounting national teacher shortage that has led to fierce competition among districts for experienced and qualified staff (Blair, 2000). In contrast to the situation in Kentucky, many Maryland school districts are large and in fairly close geographic proximity to one another, giving qualified teachers ample opportunity to find employment outside of their present district or to transfer within it.

Yet when we asked respondents to rate their preparedness for the current teaching assignment, confidence abounded. In the Kentucky sample, most teachers felt adequately prepared (34%) or very well prepared (60%). Only 6% of respondents conceded that they might lack preparation for the year's teaching assignment. The numbers in the Maryland sample were very similar. Certification for one's subjects or teaching areas appeared to be rather irrelevant for the teachers who were not fully certified: 42% of them felt "very well prepared" for their current teaching assignment. Thus, teachers overwhelmingly professed to be well or adequately prepared for their teaching assignment even though quite a number of them, particularly in the seven Maryland schools on probation, were fairly new to the profession, new in their school, and sometimes not fully certified in their field. Still, one-half of the whole sample believed that "the typical teacher at their school ranks near the top of the teaching profession in knowledge and skills." Thus, far from being tainted by their schools' designation as lacking or failing, these teachers expressed certainty about their professional quality and worth. Very few teachers from either state conceded in the anonymous survey that they might need help. Sense of competence and actual teaching experience, however, were not necessarily congruent.

Having high confidence in their own competence, teachers had a strong tendency to attribute their school's problems to external factors by translating the *school*'s low scores into low *student* performance, although some, particularly administrators and instructional specialists, criticized teachers as well. In the view of a majority of interviewees, the challenging living circumstances of the students—poverty, unstable families, drugs, high mobility, and the like—were dominant explanations for the school's decline and made it difficult for them to raise student performance:

> I don't think it is, honestly I don't think it's the teaching as much as it is the children. (10-14; first-grade teacher)

> I have to state that poverty is a great unequalizer in this, but I've never looked at poverty as an excuse . . . to not perform, because I come from poverty myself, and the expectation was always for us to perform. . . . So, that doesn't become the excuse for it. But nonetheless, you cannot overlook its pervasive impact on the learning process. (E-7; elementary school principal)

> Each year, we're getting more and more kids who bring to us less and less skills. (A-7; seventh-grade social studies teacher)

In one inner-city elementary school (School F), the schoolwide analysis of reasons for decline resulted in the identification of two problems: "First, children are disruptive and can't focus, and secondly, children are behind"(F-8).

As the causes for the schools' performance problems were largely externalized, control over them seemed doubtful. Interviewees saw some shortcomings in their schools as well (e.g., teacher turnover, high numbers of beginning and uncertified teachers, a district in disarray), and large percentages of survey respondents stated that the exertion of more effort on the part of all teachers at the school would contribute greatly to school improvement. But with the exception of instructional specialists and administrators outside the classroom, very few classroom teachers were self-critical. Instead, a defensive posture fending off the assault on one's professional reputation seemed to have taken hold.

Teachers scoffed at the punitive aspects of probation. Some were proud of having developed a special competence in surviving the difficult socioeconomic environment of their students and doing a job that not too many could be good at or even wanted to be good at. Some dared the state to replace them. A teacher in one of the first elementary schools on probation in Maryland described her feelings and reasoning in very vivid terms:

> Basically, if you think you can do it better, come in, step in, and feel free to show us how to do it any better than how we've been trying to do it. . . . They [the state] lay these threats on the table, "We're gonna come take you over." And you just get to the point where you say————. . . . You know, they came, and all the news cameras were here, and of course the only teacher that they caught on television was me, walking my children down the hall. I said, "Now every person in this state is going to say, 'There's the teacher that represents a poor and failing school.'" And I just, it was just heartbreaking because it wasn't the case, and even when the cameraman turned the camera off, he said, "How come your children weren't running down the hall?" I said, "My children don't behave that way." . . . Originally they were talking about us going back to zero-based staffing, and you'd have to reapply for your job, but I didn't, I wasn't personally concerned that I wasn't going to have a job. And plus, I knew, too, that if it wasn't here, I'd be someplace else because I wasn't outright fired. So, I wasn't that worried. I was more concerned with how bad it's going to be when we come back in the fall. Well, the feeling was, "Fine, fire me!" (E-3)

Confidence bordered on bravado when interviewees called "the state's bluff," when they doubted the effectiveness of state intervention and contrasted the poor track record of the state to their own expertise:

I could see it if the state had a good curriculum per se that they have done. Why take it over when you don't have anything to offer? What are they going to offer? (E-12)

The state can't do any better. (G-6, seventh/eighth-grade mathematics teacher)

I am anxious for someone to show us a way that we can improve, as long as it truly is an improvement on what the children are learning and able to do. And I'm not so sure what the state is using as an assessment shows, answers that. I'm not sure about that. But, personally, no, I don't have any threat. Hey, I have an ego problem. If someone thinks that they can do a better job than me, then come on and show me. I'd be anxious to learn that. (F-8)

GOOD PRESSURE

Only a small minority of respondents outright welcomed the state's intervention. They felt that accountability would be beneficial for their school as a lever for change in addition to resources. Some teachers in Maryland went as far as embracing state takeover if it brought in another force that would have to take responsibility for the affairs of the school: "I just don't see it as they would replace the teachers. It's just them saying they're taking responsibility for the school" (B-1).

It was rare that teachers reported that they had "questions . . . as far as [their] teaching and wondering if there were some things that [they] could have done that may have helped students learn more, to be better prepared for the test or if there was something that [they] did that had a backward effect or a negative effect" (20-14). With the reticence of their colleagues in mind, administrators and teachers with special assignments especially tended to welcome probation as "good pressure," like the school improvement resource teacher at School A who was one of the outright supporters of probation:

So to a certain extent, we're in kind of a fishbowl and stuff like that, but when that happens you're held accountable. You have to produce, and I was in one school just for 1 year, and there was no accountability at that school, and teachers kind of just did what they wanted, and I couldn't stay there. (A-15)

Similarly, the vice principal of an elementary school viewed the pressures of probation positively. For her, probation was not only a way for the school to obtain additional attention and resources but also a way to put faculty on notice. Yet at the same time she doubted the school's culpability for the status:

> I was not surprised at all, and I welcomed it [probation] because they need help. That's what I thought. The school needs help and what better way than to have the state people come in and try to monitor and see that everyone here is really trying to do the best job. It's not the teacher or the administrators the reason why the school is the way it is. It's because of the location and the type of population that we have. (C-6)

When teachers welcomed probation, they saw it either as a way to garner support or as a wake-up call for others. But they rarely directed such a wake-up at themselves. The following quote comes from a teacher at School G, a school that had once had a reputation for academic excellence but had recently fallen on hard times partly due to the negative impact of a change of its attendance zone. She greeted probation as a way to examine the school's standards but doubted that it would have any effect on her personally:

> It was the fact that the standards had been allowed to fall . . . very low and as a result, no, I was not at all surprised. I was quite pleased when the school was designated reconstitution-eligible. I don't think the state department or anybody else can really come into my room or some of the other rooms in this building and show me something which is going to significantly change the quality of instruction the children are receiving. I'm a good teacher, and I base that on the opinions of my colleagues, on the opinions of my parents here, of my children. I'm also pretty tough. (G-1; seventh/eighth-grade social studies teacher)

Another middle school teacher in a troubled inner-city environment hoped for the state's firm hand to shore up the authority of the school in solving a rampant discipline problem:

> Once the state comes in, hopefully, they'll put some draconian laws into effect and the students will have to fall in line. . . . I think the teachers try to maintain a certain level of decorum and education, and stuff like that, but students often feel that they can disrespect the authority figures in the school and get away with it. (D-17; social studies teacher)

In one Kentucky school with a tradition of innovation, probation was seen as a lever to rally the faculty to adopt a comprehensive school reform design, the Modern Red School House:

> There is no way we would have been able to get our faculty to buy into that program because with that program, you had to have a certain percentage of the faculty agree to participate and do what they are going to be asked to do, and our faculty probably, we just wouldn't have gotten that percentage had there not been the cloud of decline hanging over there in the background saying, "You know people are going to think that we are not doing our job. We've got to do something different." So the decline forced us to really look at ourselves and decide that something had to be changed and for us we decided to go for Modern Red. (KY 30-03; fifth-grade teacher)

Thus, teachers and administrators welcomed probation for a variety of reasons. But almost none of the supporters interpreted it as an incentive to examine their own teaching and practice. Either they associated it with external benefits or they saw it as a lever to move other people in a particular direction, the latter view being popular among administrators.

GETTING RID OF THE LABEL

Yet the stigma of being publicly identified as low-performing was personally irksome and remained an irritant that teachers strove to remove. Only 14% of the survey respondents felt indifferent about the label. Most responding teachers attached medium or high importance to raising test scores and exiting probation. But while 58% found it "very important personally that the school raise its performance," only about 40% agreed to this goal when we asked about it in terms of the states' assessments (MSPAP, KIRIS/CATS). Rather, it was a matter of teachers' and the school's prestige in the eyes of the public to get rid of the low-performance label:

> I'm a very positive person and I feel very good about what I do personally myself in my classroom, but the public doesn't see that unless you've had their child or they know you. They just see what's written in general numbers. (20-09; English teacher)

> It's important because all the county sees is the test scores. We have one of the most dynamic programs going on here, but if the scores

are not saying that we can meet the standards, we're not doing anything. (B-12; health teacher)

I want to see our school look good to the district. I don't want our school to look so bad because we're not that bad. I mean, our scores might show it, but we're not that bad. (40-02; eighth-grade English teacher)

Teachers rarely embedded the raising of test scores in a broader vision of school improvement. Very few teachers went as far as this fourth-grade teacher from a small town in Kentucky, for whom "it [was] not about the numbers" but about the "work and the effort and the focus that [the school would] get from having to bring the scores up" (30-04). The prevailing sentiment was that raising test scores and overcoming probation was primarily "a prestige thing."

COMMITMENT TO STAY

Teachers can exit probation in two ways: They can strive toward raising test scores for the whole school or they can leave the labeled school. Once a school is publicly identified as low-performing, it is eminently important for successful school improvement that high-quality teachers be retained or attracted. It is conceivable that a probation designation may invigorate the commitment of teachers to the organization as they take up the challenge of public rebuke. Alternatively, teachers may loose hope, may fear additional pressures, or may resent having their own professional reputation or self-worth tarnished by the school's probation stigma. It would have serious negative repercussions for a school's prospects for improvement if probation accelerated faculty turnover and if it drove out the "wrong" teachers—that is, those most strongly motivated by the accountability system.

We grouped survey respondents into three levels of commitment. Highly committed teachers expressed the intention of either staying put or staying put through the improvement process. Uncertain teachers envisioned staying perhaps for another year, while teachers who wished to leave were categorized as uncommitted to their school. Overall, about half of all respondents expressed a definite commitment to staying at the school, about a fifth were uncertain, and between a fourth and a third were ready to move. Teachers in Kentucky schools were more committed to their school than Maryland respondents: 59% from Kentucky as opposed to 46% in Maryland expressed certainty. With only half of a faculty being certain to stay, commitment to the organization was a precious commodity in these schools, particularly across the seven Maryland schools. The figures from Maryland matched a real yearly teacher turnover rate of up to 50% in many of the seven schools during the study period. But even for the four Kentucky schools, it is not clear whether the higher commitment was defined positively or negatively (as lack of exit options).

We asked survey respondents to rate the importance of a number of reasons for staying or leaving. The ones committed to staying liked the administration, colleagues, and students, but they were also hopeful for improvement of their school and accepted the challenge of "proving that [they] are better than it appears"(see Table 1.1). Apparently the highly committed had an appreciation of their school and believed in its prospects, but they also kept a distance from the verdicts of the accountability system. Positive energy at school as a result of probation was relatively less important a reason for staying but was nevertheless named by more than half in the 11 schools. Thus, responding teachers committed to their probationary school seemed to be stirred by the designation but less swayed by actual positive reverberations of the new status.

Reasons for leaving differed by state (see Table 1.2). In the Kentucky sample, respondents' strongest reason for leaving was pressure due to the

Table 1.1. Reasons for Staying at Current Job (rank order)

Rank	Maryland	Rank	Kentucky
1	I have great hope for the school (91%)	1	I like my colleagues (95%)
2	I like the students (89%)	2	I like the administration (92%)
3	We will prove we are better than it appears (85%)	3	I like the students (89%)
		4	We will prove we are better than it appears (88%)
4	I like my colleagues (82%)		
4	I like the administration (82%)	4	I have great hope for the school (88%)
5	I play an important role for this community (66%)	5	I have friends here (83%)
		6	I play an important role for this community (71%)
6	Probation has greatly energized this school (61%).		
		7	Probation has greatly energized this school (56%)
7	I have friends here (60%)		
8	The school is close to my home (56%)	8	The school is close to my home (38%)
9	I have no other option at this point (21%)	9	I have no other option at this point (17%)
10	I am too close to retirement to change schools (18%)	10	I am too close to retirement to change schools (13%)

Notes: Rank based on percentage answering each item as "Very important" or "Important." *N*'s for the seven Maryland schools ranged from 148 to 159; *N*'s for the four Kentucky schools ranged from 82 to 90.

Table 1.2. Reasons for Leaving Current Job (rank order)

Rank	Maryland	Rank	Kentucky
1	I have better career options elsewhere (67%)	1	I am tired of the additional pressure probation has put on this school (73%)
2	The school feels like a sinking ship (62%)	2	The students here wear me down (72%)
2	I can get higher pay elsewhere (62%)	3	My work is unappreciated by the community (63%)
3	This district is not a place where one can be successful as a teacher (59%)	4	This district is not a place where one can be successful as a teacher (60%)
4	I am tired of the additional pressure probation has put on this school (57%)	5	The school feels like a sinking ship (58%)
5	You cannot count on teachers here (51%)	6	You cannot count on teachers here (47%)
5	The students here wear me down (51%)	7	I have better career options elsewhere (40%)
6	My work is unappreciated by the community (47%)	8	I do not like the administration (37%)
6	I do not like the administration (47%)	9	I can get higher pay elsewhere (33%)
7	I will retire this year (12%)	10	I will retire this year (20%)

Notes: Rank based on percentage answering each item as "Very important" or "Important." N's for the seven Maryland schools ranged from 97 to 108; N's for the four Kentucky schools ranged from 64 to 81.

probationary status of the school, followed by disappointment with students, community, and district. Exit options, on the other hand, played less of a role as reasons for leaving. Among Maryland teachers, reasons for leaving were weighted differently. Here, exit options (i.e., other career options and higher pay elsewhere) stood out as the most important reason for leaving, in addition to the school feeling "like a sinking ship." The pressures of probation were of lesser importance. As noted earlier, career opportunities were most likely more plentiful in the booming Washington–Baltimore corridor, where the seven Maryland schools were located, than in the Kentucky locations. It is conceivable that disenchanted Maryland respondents would have felt more pressure from probation if they had had fewer exit options. Alternatively, it is conceivable that increased exit options could have decreased overall commitment in the four Kentucky schools and attenuate the perception of pressure from probation. The patterns from the two states suggest that exit options might act as a valve to relieve the pressures of probation.

In the interviews, the most frequent reasons given for staying were the feeling of being needed, supportive colleagues and administrators, convenience, hope that the school would be successful, and the potential for professional growth. Similarly to survey responses, interviewees were eager to refute the notion that they were at their job site by default, trapped in low-performing schools not unlike their students. Many stressed that they could pursue other options but consciously chose to stay at their school:

> I could easily go anywhere else. I'm a Black male, science. I get job offers all the time. . . . I think that there's a need for me here. I really do and that's one reason why I became a teacher. Teaching to me is like ministry. If you don't really feel that way about it, you need to get a check somewhere else, probably for more money. My wife's income allows me to do this, to be a teacher. It's not for everyone. If you don't have the kids' best interests in mind, then teaching is not for you. It's a little selfish on my part because I want to have a better society and this is one of the ways that I can impact society. I have a baby. I wonder where she'll go to school, what kind of people she'll have to deal with. That's why I'm here, to cut a role for my family and these young people. (40-15; sixth-grade science teacher)

But others, especially novice teachers, expressed exhaustion and a desire to move on, despite feeling needed:

> I think these 2 years have really worn me out. And I think I want to expand. I've really learned a love for the educational field and for these kids. I'm not sure that the classroom is the best place for me. . . . I've really been run down by a lot of things that I don't feel like I can control in the classroom. (F-20; third-grade mathematics teacher)

For some interviewees, staying at their school was connected with sacrifice and endurance, as for this social studies department head in a Maryland middle school:

> I'm a stakeholder. These are our kids. These are our problems. You deal with it. And, granted, it's not always the most positive, but life wasn't always promised to be easy. And you deal with it. (A-7)

Especially in the middle schools, complaints about student discipline were widespread and senior teachers had to learn to develop a certain hardiness to last in the challenging environment of their schools:

> It's a tough place to work. . . . The problems that we have with some of these students are overwhelming. You really have to lay the law down. I've been around here for quite a while, so I survive here, but for a young teacher to come in here for the first time, first year, it's

probably too much, and I've seen them come and go. . . . I'm used to this kind of war zone. I've thought about putting in transfers over the years, but something always happens to make me change my mind. (40-07; eighth-grade social studies teacher)

A younger teacher in the same school described how he had learned to endure this "war zone":

My first year here I was physically assaulted three times. I was assaulted this year already. But I think as you're here longer, the kids respect you a little more. . . . My first year, all the kids were like, "Well, we got rid of three plus the subs, we'll get rid of you." It was very difficult my first year and then I went through [a teacher preparation program] at the same time, but I was determined that I was going to do it. When I came back the second year, it was like I was an old-timer. In the kids' eyes, you've been here forever. Every year it's gotten a lot easier. (40-12; art teacher)

This teacher's endurance was remarkable in light of the actual turnover in the schools, especially in the Maryland schools. Many teachers expressed unwillingness to tolerate these kinds of conditions for a long time, and many of those who indicated the desire to leave bemoaned the lack of discipline in their schools as a primary reason.

In some schools, probation reportedly triggered a wave of transfers, though it is hard to substantiate the contribution of probation to an overall high teacher turnover rate. While interviewees themselves rarely gave probation as the sole reason why they would want to leave their school, they were sure that some of their colleagues were leaving or had already left because of it:

There was a mass exodus out of our building, a lot of people saw [probation as] . . . an opportunity for people to come in and scrutinize what we were doing. You know, the old "under the microscope thing," and because of that a lot of people did leave. Because, in fact to be real honest with you, that's what people are even saying this year. People want to transfer out because they decided they don't want to be in a reconstitution-eligible school. (A-6; eighth-grade mathematics teacher)

This eighth-grade mathematics teacher herself also decided to leave. But she stated it was not because of probation, but because of disagreements with her principal. A teacher from School B who decided to stay described the situation in this way:

Many teachers, especially teachers who've been on the battlefield for a while, are just not real comfortable with the extra stress. You know, teaching itself has a lot of demands. And anybody who's an effective teacher generally, on a good day, goes home tired. And so, with the added stress of, "Oh, the state is here," I mean, you know, there's some added stress to being recon-eligible. . . . I just love this school. But there are teachers who are not willing to go through that fire. (B-7; sixth-grade mathematics teacher)

The most frequently cited reason for leaving, for novices and seasoned teachers alike, was that the work stress at their school had simply become too high and the rewards too low:

Let me say this. I believe in being honest. I will take [a transfer], and it's not because of administration, and it's not because of our students. I really feel that anywhere, the situation right now, where it's going to take so much, so much work, and I'm trying to focus on having certain programs at your school, and then all these extra things. It's going to be overwhelming for a lot of people, especially for myself, because I have a family. (C-2; guidance counselor)

It was striking to us that educators were prepared to leave regardless of their role or level of involvement in the school. We encountered a desire to leave among novice teachers frustrated with their teaching as much as among school improvement team members, department heads, school improvement plan writers, and administrators who were instrumental in their school's improvement process. For people in positions of responsibility, a combination of reasons came together: career advancement, better options elsewhere, disagreements with the administration, feelings of powerlessness in the face of the school's downward trend, and a general sense of being overburdened. The probationary status of their school was stated infrequently as a reason by this group. Some highly involved teachers explicitly denied that probation had anything to do with their decision or desire to leave. In schools where probation was high-profile, the school's status influenced highly involved teachers indirectly. Many resented additional pressures due to probation, such as the requirement for daily lesson plans, expanded record keeping, more supervision, new programs, and so on. Ms. S., the English department head in School A, explained her reasons for leaving in this way:

My contract very clearly states that we are to attend, required to attend two faculty staff meetings outside of school hours, per month. And I am currently attending six. And I've been trying to figure out why, for the past couple of weeks. And I'm really not a complainer. I'm not in the union. I'm not part of the Teachers Association. But it started kind of affecting me a little bit, just in terms of, you can't quite split yourself up into all these different ways. . . . You know, it's just a lot to ask when you don't seem to be compensated, and that starts to make a teacher somewhat bitter. . . . And I'm not a bitter person, I mean . . . I'm not even, it's not even recognition. It's really a situation where, "OK, I could get this done, but you know, working for peanuts here." Maybe I wouldn't be complaining about having to go get folders from Staples to do an extra workshop, if you know, my check. . . . Things like that really start to affect your motivation. It starts to affect how much commitment you want to have. . . . You know, if I could leave this building next week, I would leave at this point. (A-16)

In summary, a serious teacher commitment problem existed across the 11 schools. Probation was the number-one reason for teachers to leave in the four Kentucky schools. Teachers drew a connection between turnover and probation, but many other factors seemed to play a role in the decision to leave, prominently among them exit options and a general sense of crisis in the school. School-site conditions were key factors associated with higher commitment. Our data cannot conclusively answer whether probation drives the "wrong" teachers out of the schools. But evidence from both the qualitative and quantitative data so far suggests that highly motivated and skillful teachers were as prone to leave as their less engaged and skillful colleagues. Probation did capture the imagination of some highly motivated teachers, who responded positively to performance pressures, but it also turned many of them off.

The case of Ms. S., quoted above, is typical for teachers' ambivalent response to the pressures of probation. Ms. S., a young African American woman who attained the position of department head early in her career, at first accepted the challenge of probation out of a sense of commitment to her school. Hoping for new support, she decided to be positive. Although there was no question in her mind that the label was an affront to her personal performance and competence, probation was not an immediate reason to leave the school. Rather, she became very active as one of the school leaders. But the added stress of improvement activities, on top of an already stressful work situation that was short of rewards anyway and had become even more negative as a result of probation, made her wish to leave eventually. For many teachers, the wish to leave is not carried out, but, not unlike a large percentage of surveyed teachers, Ms. S. ended up taking a job elsewhere—in her case, due to her qualifications, in a neighboring district that offered higher pay and better working conditions.

CHAPTER 2

The Meaningfulness of Accountability

WHY THE PRESSURES OF PROBATION triggered an ambivalent response among teachers is explained further in the context of their beliefs about the accountability system. The motivational force of probation should be greatly enhanced when educators find the accountability system meaningful. Accountability is meaningful when teachers see the system as a valid and fair gauge of their own performance and as a realistic expression of their own ambitious expectations for their students. Under these conditions, they are likely to internalize the system's judgment reflected in the low-performance label and link the system's quantitative goals, standards, and assessments to their own work. In this chapter, we examine whether this internalization has occurred by looking at teachers' beliefs about the validity, fairness, and realism of the accountability system.

VALIDITY OF STATE ASSESSMENTS

Both the Maryland and Kentucky accountability systems have as a centerpiece an ambitious test that, in its emphasis on writing and higher-order thinking skills, challenges traditional teachers to change the instructional format of their classes. The concept of validity captures the degree to which teachers believe that these tests adequately assess the quality of their teaching. After all, it is adults, rather than students, who receive performance scores from the accountability system. We assume that if teachers held the tests in high esteem, if they considered the tests as valid indicators of teaching quality and effort and as tools of self-assessment, then attaining higher test scores would be more intrinsically motivating. It may be necessary for teachers to make this connection in order to incorporate new pedagogical elements into their ingrained way of teaching.

Teachers in the 11 schools on probation held a dim view of the validity of the two states' central assessments. On the survey, only small proportions of respondents from either state (Maryland, 20%; Kentucky, 10%) deemed the states' core assessments as highly valid instruments for measuring teaching quality (see Appendix for validity scale). Almost a third (31%) disagreed that "a good teacher need not fear the test." Only 22% agreed that "the test [MSPAP, KIRIS/CATS] assesses all the things that [the teacher personally] find[s] important for students to learn." Only a fourth agreed that "the test reflects just plain good teaching." Responding Kentucky teachers were even more skeptical than those from Maryland. Why this skepticism? Teachers, we found, assessed themselves with criteria that differed from those suggested by the accountability system. For many of them, there was a mismatch between their students' educational needs and what the assessments supposedly asked them to emphasize in their classrooms. They felt rewarded as teachers when they successfully tapped into those needs. High test scores paled by comparison.

Self-Assessment

Instead of referring to the state assessments, the majority of teachers in the 11 schools concentrated on interpersonal relationships and the direct experience of the classroom as primary tools for self-evaluation. Quantitative test scores rated very low as a means of establishing a sense of success. Teachers in our sample were clearly not data-driven, as Table 2.1 indicates.

To begin with, the system's quantitative performance goals and teachers' own educational goals diverged. Preparing students for a productive life was teachers' primary mission, a goal that, according to many study participants, could not be captured adequately by test scores:

Table 2.1. Indicators of Success in One's Own Teaching (rank order)

Rank	Maryland	Rank	Kentucky
1	Lively participation of class (482)	1	Answers from individual students (238)
2	Students complete tasks (479)	2	Students complete tasks (237)
3	Answers from individual students (422)	3	Lively participation of class (199)
4	Positive comments from parents (336)	4	Positive comments from parents (144)
5	High test scores on teacher-made test (290)	5	High test scores on teacher-made test (110)
6	Affection from students (232)	6	I just know it in my heart (78)
7	Praise from colleagues (185)	7	Praise from colleagues (76)
8	Maryland Functional Tests scores (179)	7	KIRIS/CATS scores (76)
9	MSPAP scores (177)	8	Praise from principal (59)
10	Praise from principal (174)	9	CTBS scores (49)
11	I just know it in my heart (166)	10	Affection from students (40)

Note: The numbers in parentheses reflect both the number of respondents choosing each item and the weight given by them.

It is not that important for me to increase the MSPAP scores. It is important for me that the kids leave here knowing more than what they did coming in. . . . I've never been a good test taker and I think that it's not a true measure of a person. A true measure of a person is a lifetime of experiences, and a test will never measure that. (B-1; seventh-grade English teacher)

I'm not anti-test, but I'm also . . . I mean, if I don't get something that should be addressed by MSPAP because I'm teaching my students an important life lesson, I'm sorry, but that life lesson [is more important], and maybe some way or somehow it will apply to MSPAP. (C-3; first-grade teacher)

In the interviews, teachers espoused goals that in their minds were at the same time more basic, more far-reaching, more substantive, and more authentic than what the tests measured:

If I can teach my children how to write appropriate, you know, a correct sentence with punctuation, capitalization . . . how to figure out their math problem, how to be able to be critical thinkers . . . I mean, that to me is more important than the state test. (G-17)

Just getting these kids to do their best and be able to write and to answer questions, that's my key priority. I want to see these kids being able to answer questions, do the higher-level thinking questions, be able to have a conversation with someone, be able to get along with a classmate, without putting them down or calling them names. (B-7)

As a result, whether students grasped the teacher's own curriculum, supposedly tailored to the needs of the students, was a more meaningful criterion for effectiveness than students' mastery of an external test:

Looking at the kids' background, and looking at what is written in that test and how it addresses them and the social issues that they have, they may not make that connection. So, they may not do well. But what is important to me is if my kids are learning the things that I'm teaching them, somehow they're able to connect it to the things that they're doing. (A-8; eighth-grade social studies teacher)

Personal educational goals contrasted with the importance of "prestige" and public reputation as an externally imposed concern. A number of interviewees discussed this contrast as a split between the professional and personal:

> My success is to have students achieve. . . . Personally? No, [the test is not important.] But I know on a professional basis it has to, which is where I have to gear my lesson plans. I mean, many things I do in class are geared toward the MSPAP. I don't necessarily agree with that, but I do work toward that. So in a sense, yes, I do see achievement as that, but it's not my own personal achievement, it's my professional sort of you have to do this thing. (G-2; social studies teacher)

> To me personally, my thought on the tests and the whole process, it's not that important because I know what these kids are learning, and I think I know what we need to be teaching. But to me, professionally and to the staff, and for the image that it gives us it's very important, very important. (30-01; elementary school principal)

Despite this incongruity between teachers' valued curriculum and state assessments, accountability was not rejected altogether. Those who embraced the idea of accountability were nevertheless doubtful about the test-driven nature of the system, such as this eighth-grade special education teacher in a Maryland middle school:

> If I had a child, I'd want my teacher and principal to be accountable for when I see something wrong. . . . But . . . I can't be 100% focused on it, you know. And I still consider myself a pretty good instructor . . . I'm more interested in each one of my students to be citizens. I am not at all interested in numbers. I do think numbers have their place, and I do believe that they can . . . show you where you are. However, to label the student because of those numbers, I think, is unfair. (B-10)

Interviewees professed to teach to the test, even though, as this sixth-grade English teacher from Kentucky phrased it, "I don't agree and maybe I don't feel like [it], but I'm trying to give them what they need in order to pass those tests, to be prepared" (40-11). But regardless of compliance with the test, good teaching was not necessarily reflected in good test scores:

> I do teach to the standards that are set forth by the board and I try to meet each one of those standards. . . . If you're a good teacher you'll be successful in your classroom no matter what a standardized test says. (40-02; eighth-grade English teacher)

Even some of those who apparently had mastered the system's teaching standards felt a sense of alienation in this test-driven accountability environment. Apparently, internalizing external performance standards was difficult in a system that seemingly worked against teachers rather than with them, as this seventh-grade mathematics teacher explained:

> It's more important for me to meet my students' needs. And that's not always easy because administration can be intolerable, and state and district can be a bit intolerable . . . I don't see the care for the teachers. I just don't. I'm like, if you want to reach the kids, how about reaching us? And we're the ones that have to get to them. You have to get to us. They can't get to students, state and district can't get to students. How? They're not here day to day. . . . That's the odd thing. People have visited my classroom and I've been congratulated, I've been rewarded, I've been applauded, you know. They raved about my classroom, and I'm like, why? And for the most part it is because I know the inside. I know how to meet state and district standards. In other words, I know how to implement what they want. I know how to teach that way. I know how to make it look as if, you know, this is going on, and not to say that I'm not, but I know what's going on underneath as well, you know? My room is always set up the way it's supposed to be. My kids are writing in math. I have the work published, you know, every few weeks. I have my [daily lesson plans] ready. I just started performance tasks with them, so they're doing cooperative learning, so yes. It appears as if I'm meeting state standards, but in my heart of hearts, I cannot get a part of myself. I just don't feel it, because, it's, I'm doing it and I don't know how I'm doing it. It's like, OK, I must be running on fumes. (B-09; seventh-grade mathematics teacher)

On the other hand, there were those who saw the tests as integrated into their way of teaching and as indicators of good teaching. Often an avowed minority in their schools, they were more commonly staff with special assignments than ordinary classroom teachers:

> If you've been teaching, "Open your books to page da da da," you know, you're going to be stressed. And administration is stressed . . . when the reports come out, . . . and from that point on you get yelled out for the rest of the year. Less stress, you know, take some preventative measures. Get rid of those textbooks for a while and start a little more hands-on things. You won't be as stressed. (B-10; mathematics specialist)

The more prevailing view was that teachers were already doing "the best they can." This, however, did not mean that they deflected all criticism or denied all blemish as far as their teaching was concerned. In the interviews, some teachers, though not the majority, judged themselves quite conscientiously at times. Conflicts with individual students, the inability to control one's classes or to compel students to work, not reaching one's lowest-achieving students at all, or not making any progress despite repeated attempts at reteaching were grounds for interviewees to doubt their effectiveness as teachers, in the face of which data-driven diagnostics paled in significance. Stories from classrooms were related with a tinge of frustration, sometimes helplessness, or even victimization—for example, in the case of the teachers in one Maryland school who used to pray together in the morning for strength to make it through the day. Novice teachers, represented in large numbers in most Maryland schools on probation, were particularly preoccupied with day-to-day survival in the classroom. But such preoccupation was not restricted to that group.

Student Needs

Most teachers saw basic skills, disciplined conduct, and citizenship skills, said to be needed by students to secure later employment, as the goals of the educational process and the criteria according to which to judge one's teaching effort. Modeling appropriate social behavior, insisting on good work habits, and transmitting basic knowledge loomed as tasks in the face of which concerns about poor test scores faded. Many teachers aspired to teaching higher-order thinking skills and performance-based activities, prominently featured in the two state tests. But they also sensed a gap between the test format and the needs of their students, presumably lying in the area of basic skill development and often within a range far below the grade level the test was geared to:

> I think I'm very good at what I do. . . . I think the concept of the test is very good, and you know, it's important because I want my students to have those skills. I think the state needs to . . . realize that you have to take children where they are and you can't . . . always work a miracle, you know. (A-2; eighth-grade science teacher)

Teachers repeatedly bemoaned that the MSPAP or the KIRIS/CATS tests were "too hard" for their students, leaving them at a loss as to how to bridge the gap. The instructional specialist in one of the inner-city elementary schools in Maryland described her dilemma this way:

What was so frustrating was, the state is telling us this, but yet the teacher assessments of the children's performance is much different. So, you have your teachers saying, "Well look, this is what I'm supposed to teach. This is what I taught. This is what the child can now do." (F-8)

Several teachers related stories that illustrated the perceived gap:

One year I gave the test to a group of . . . fifth graders, and they were to read, it was a social studies aspect part of the test. And after reading, going through the material, many students felt completely overwhelmed, "There's no way I can read all of this, form a graph, and write about it in 30 minutes." And so, some of my brightest students put their heads on their desks and began to sob. (E-7)

The presumed misfit between student needs in the area of basic skills and the highly ambitious goals of the accountability system in the area of higher-order thinking was discussed in both the Maryland and Kentucky interviews, but it was accentuated in the Maryland schools. Here, teachers felt confronted with the task of balancing perceived student learning needs with tests that emphasized both basic skills (MFTs, Comprehensive Test of Basic Skills [CTBS]) and higher-order thinking and social skills (MSPAP), the latter on a highly ambitious achievement level. One instructional specialist described the differences in mathematics this way:

You are going to see the disconnect. . . . When they take the functional test, they are literally working out problems and filling in what they think the answer is. The only way to get a math score off of MSPAP is if a child has written a paragraph about how he did a problem. No formulas or anything mathematical is scored for MSPAP. It is their writing about whatever they did. (B-20; instructional specialist)

The existence of the basic skills tests validated basic skills instruction in the eyes of many interviewees.

As a result, teachers expressed ambivalence about taking directions from the accountability system. On one hand, in reasserting their competence, only 14% of the survey respondents were not "exactly sure what [their] students are expected to do on the tests [MSPAP, KIRIS/CATS]." And the overwhelming majority stated that they were guided by the system. But, on the other hand, only about half agreed that the system told them "what is most important for the school to accomplish" and that the "accountability goals provide a focus for [their] teaching efforts."

Rewards

Against the abstractness of summary scores and numbers, interviewees maintained a focus on the individual child as the quintessence of teaching and the source of reward and satisfaction:

> I don't feel like I need to know that they think that I'm doing the best at this and they're going to reward me for this or whatever. That's just not really important to me. I like to see my students succeed and I like to think that yes, I had something to do with that. Really, that's the only reason why we're here. The other people aren't that important. It's our students that we help make some achievements. (40-04; sixth-grade reading teacher)

Interacting with children, feeling needed, making a difference in somebody's life, and being stimulated by the nonroutine nature of the work were the prime motivators for interviewed teachers to work at their schools:

> I really feel that these children need me, and I have come to realize over the last 13 years that I need them a lot more than they do me. And I can shut out everything else except the children. There have been days I would have liked to have had a chute that shot me from my car right up the wall into my window and I wouldn't have had to see anybody else. [Laughter] Those days pass too. [Laughter] . . . [It's] these children, the children. (20-25)

The most frequent reward cited was the occasional appreciation teachers received from individual students, often related in moving stories, such as the following one told by a teacher in one of Maryland's first schools on probation:

> At Christmastime I was really feeling really low because I felt this doubt that all the behavior problems that I have in my class—I'm not getting through and it doesn't seem right to me my children are passing my tests and my quizzes. My standards are kind of high, and some of my kids can meet them and some of them cannot meet them. I don't get to work with the lower achievers like I want to, and I felt really like I don't want to come back to school after Christmas. And so one of my students made me a card, a Christmas card, and she kept telling me, "Ms. M., make sure you read this, make sure you read this." And when I got home, I took all these little letters, love letters I call them, and I was going to throw all of them away because

I just felt like giving up at that time. And so I pulled hers out. I was going to throw it in the trash. And I said, "No, I have to read this." And so I told my husband, I said, "One of my students gave me this." And so I was opening it up and it said, she said, "Dear Ms. M., I wish you a Merry Christmas to you and your family and a Happy New Year and thank you very much for what you have taught me this year. I have learned a lot." And I stood in the middle of the floor and I started to cry, and my husband gave me a hug, and my daughter gave me a hug, and my daughter, she was crying because of me crying. And that's what made me feel like at least somebody appreciates what I'm doing. (E-16)

The pathos with which these stories were told betrays the infrequency of their occurrence and the dearth of these kinds of rewards in a teacher's life. Teachers in the 11 schools described their work as frustrating and devoid of external rewards and recognition, yet meaningful and stimulating:

I don't think middle school teachers are given enough credit and recognition for the job that they do. . . . We are dealing with a very complicated age group, and it is a hard job. I like working with young people. I've always liked working with young people. It's a challenge. It's never the same. You're always learning. Even though it's been years and years, it's just always changing. (G-15; guidance counselor)

For some, this orientation toward the individual student was coupled with a sense of commitment to the community. Many of the interviewed teachers in Maryland are African Americans who felt a sense of affiliation with the African American communities that surround the selected schools. Some interviewees said they chose to dedicate themselves to this particularly needy group of at-risk students, such as the dean of discipline at an inner-city middle schools:

When I was in school, I didn't have anyone; I was a knucklehead just like the rest of them. And I didn't have anyone to kind of push me along. . . . I feel like I have to be here because I never know when a student's going to come to school needing me for something. (D-24; dean of discipline)

Some teachers saw teaching in difficult circumstances as a religious calling, a theme that strongly surfaced in a number of Kentucky interviews:

I guess for me it's a little bit different. I've felt like for this job, I don't know if this is going to be appropriate for your study, but I felt like God wanted me to be working with kids that had bigger needs than, you know, an average classroom, and I prayed about and I had other offers to teach other places, and I really felt like this would be somewhere that I could use my talents to hopefully make a difference in a bigger way than just a normal classroom because they are lacking in so many just basic ways of nurturing and things like that. . . . What's frustrating for me is not really that we are . . . necessarily missing out on the reward, in the fact that it's monetary; [it] really doesn't make a big difference to me but . . . I feel like it's not fair to our kids. (KY 10-09; first-grade teacher)

For senior teachers who were dedicating their lives to teaching, the short-term reward of higher test scores or reward money paled against the long-term reward of having made a contribution to children's lives:

I'm based on future rewards that some day these kids are going to find me walking down the mall . . . and I'm going to say, "What are you doing with your life?" "Oh, I'm a doctor or I'm a truck driver, I'm something." And I'll say, "Oh yes, I had a little piece of that." I had a little hand in shaping that. So, I guess that's really, that's the only reward you get. (G-5; science teacher)

I've been lucky enough to have been here so long I now have children of children. And it makes you feel good, it makes you feel good when they come back and they're in college or they get elected to the state senate as one of my students just did. (G-15; guidance counselor)

Thus, teachers in the interviews affirmed that theirs was a stressful and challenging, yet meaningful, job, but they doubted that parents, the wider public, and the distant state authorities appreciated their toil. Teaching under the circumstances in which many probationary schools found themselves, many interviewees held, was short on external rewards. Probation was just "one more thing that . . . we get smacked on the wrist that says, no, you didn't do a good job"(40-04; sixth-grade reading teacher), when in fact "the ones that don't receive [rewards] actually need [them] more" (40-13; seventh-grade social studies teacher).

Low salaries were mentioned as a symptom of society's disrespect for teaching, particularly for teaching in poor communities, where salaries are even lower. These low salaries, interviewees argued, proved that teachers could not possibly be motivated by financial rewards: "I'm not here just to get a paycheck; teachers don't make that much money, you know, so it's not about the money" (B-2; Spanish teacher). Similarly, a principal of a Kentucky elementary school who "had a business one time" where he "was making $100 an hour, making furniture and . . . couldn't even motivate [him]self to give up a fishing trip to go work and make that money" (KY 10-12). Interviewees appreciated money, but it did not "float their boat."

In summary, we saw earlier that educators in the study tended to value the achievement of accountability goals as a means to lift the public stigma. We see here that educators, to large degree, rejected the tests as valid indicators of teaching quality. Not having met the quantitative performance expectations of the system, they defined performance success in different terms. Against the fixation on quantitative performance goals within the accountability system, they held the value of personalization. Seeing themselves as the ones in close proximity to the students, they diagnosed a misfit between external performance criteria and the internal needs of their students. While some contended that the learning needs of their students called for basic skill development, others wanted to find a bridge to higher-order thinking skills. But very few judged the tests to be the appropriate bridges. In the Maryland schools, basic skills and performance-based pedagogy were almost seen as dichotomous.

Teachers' internal performance standards were not congruent with external accountability standards. Many teachers' self-concept rejected the image of the score maximizer in favor of the image of an educator dedicated to the intellectual and social growth of individual students and committed to the needs of the local community. Likewise, rewards were derived from encounters with individual students or learning groups and from psychic satisfaction. This contrasted with the dearth of rewards that could be derived from the external environment of the school. In the eyes of many, probation proved this point. Thus, teachers were led away from the accountability system when actualizing their internal norms and standards of teaching. However, lifting the public stigma of failure was a strong incentive for teachers to comply with the test despite misgivings about the tests' validity.

FAIRNESS OF THE ACCOUNTABILITY SYSTEM

While the concept of validity hones in on the congruence between official and personal standards and (self-) assessments, the concept of fairness emphasizes teachers' feelings about the rightfulness of the system's classifications, its labels, and the judgments implied in them. The strength of teacher discontent with the system's fairness was striking. Teachers who thought that the accountability system was unfair strongly predominated (see the *fairness* scale in the Appendix). In terms of single items, 61% of respondents felt "unfairly judged by the accountability system." Only 9% disagreed with the notion that "the accountability system is stacked against poor schools," and 85% rejected the system's accountability verdict, insisting that they were "working to [their] best ability and effort despite the low scores the school received." Clearly, the accountability system was not considered a fair judgment on teacher performance according to a great majority. Not surprisingly, teachers who possessed more confidence in their own skills and knowledge were more likely to think that the accountability system was unfair.

In the interviews, accountability as a general idea was widely accepted. The state had the right to utilize an external test to measure school performance, and since the state chose to select these specific tests, it behooved teachers to pay attention to them. Some explicitly asserted the authoritativeness of the system:

> Anything that's for [the] benefit of the students . . . I trusted the state . . . has looked into it further and felt that we needed to be reconstituted, then, you know, I'm in agreement with it. (G-11; middle school mathematics teacher)

> If the label, if there's a criteria in place and if the school has not met with that set of criteria, then it's fair that the label be there. (G-3; seventh/eighth-grade science teacher, department chair, school improvement team chair)

Yet most interviewees rejected the verdict of probation as unfair, even though they might have acknowledged the reality of low test scores and welcomed the resources given to the school. A number of arguments for the unfairness of the tests recurred across the two states. The tests did not reflect teachers' efforts in dealing with the difficult socioeconomic environment of the students, the difficulty levels of the tests were inappropriate for the many students below grade level, and the year-to-year testing of student cohorts ("comparing apples and oranges") did not control for rapid demographic changes and varying levels of students' academic preparedness. Some of these arguments, previously discussed, referred to the lack of validity and lack of control over test score development.

Most ubiquitous were arguments related to the socioeconomic background of students:

> I feel that they are picking on [School D] because we are in the neighborhood that we're in. . . . Initially when we were termed

reconstitution-eligible, it was known that we were also in an area where the homicide rate was the highest of all the areas of [the city]. We're also in an area of a lot of unemployment, and we have a lot of parents who have substance abuse problems, so they did not look at all of the contributing factors to our low test scores and our low attendance. They just labeled us reconstitution-eligible. (D-23; elementary school curriculum specialist)

I kind of think that the comparisons done with that are a little bit unfair for us because I am familiar with a lot of the other schools in our district. I have children in this district that don't go to school here. Judging from what they get as far as home participation and attendance and all of that, that to me plays a big part in what our success can be. Those are things that some of us don't have any control over here. We can't make them come to school, and if we don't get parents' support, then we're obviously not going to get that either. (KY 40-04; sixth-grade reading teacher)

Interviewees resoundingly rejected the procedure by which cohorts from previous years are used as a baseline to measure performance improvements in subsequent years. Teachers argued that this was invalid and especially unfair for schools with an urban character:

I mean, if you look at how transient [District A] and [District B] are, and I'm sure . . . that's a major factor, that makes me question the validity of the test. The test itself, I think the ideas are good, but the actual using it as a measuring tool with so much, so much pressure, I don't feel that it's aimed at urban schools, because you have kids that change schools six times in 3 years, or more than that. You get really downtown, you have kids that change schools twice a year for their whole elementary school life. How can you hold a principal and their teachers accountable to *that* situation? (G-6; seventh/eighth-grade mathematics teacher)

This transience could also explain the frequent fluctuations of test scores from year to year that plagued almost all of the 11 schools, bolstering the view that the tests were insensitive to teachers' efforts in urban schools, given that "the teachers have all been here for years, so it can't be teacher change" (B-14; sixth-grade science teacher).

Indeed, a number of schools encountered shifts in their populations that the calculations of either accountability system ignored. Two schools had recently suffered from district magnet school policies that designated them as neighborhood schools and had caused a drain of top students to other schools. One school had encountered changes in the economy of the neighborhood that made it a less convenient drop-off point for parents from middle-class neighborhoods. Two schools had seen a steep increase in the proportion of special education students. Four schools had seen a major redrawing of attendance zones, sometimes for the better, sometimes for the worse.

In summary, the great majority of teachers from the 11 schools doubted the fairness of the probation verdict. They questioned either the technical accuracy of the measures that identified them as low-performing or the adequacy of the tests for their specific work situation, which in most cases was a school that served students from lower socioeconomic strata of society. Most teachers felt that rather than being rewarded for the challenges that this situation entails, the accountability system added insult to injury. Although the feeling was widespread that the accountability system was a fact that needed to be taken seriously for the sake of students and the school's external standing, the system did not tap into deeper layers of teachers' values. Large numbers of teachers in the 11 schools refused to internalize the judgment of their accountability agency. Instead, they felt "picked on."

REALISM OF ACCOUNTABILITY GOALS

On the survey, a large majority of respondents expressed doubts about their school being able to reach the official standards. On the realism scale (see Appendix), only 6% (Kentucky) to 14% (Maryland) thought the accountability goals were very realistic. Almost 50% of the Kentucky respondents believed that the goals were very unrealistic. Respondents were more hopeful for incremental improvements of their schools.

Ignoring the high-performance demands of the accountability system, teachers in both the Maryland and Kentucky schools commonly emphasized accomplishing learning increments of any size in their students. They were not "worried about the 70% or whatever satisfactory they need to be at. If they can improve 5%, 10%, they're improving, they're increasing" (B-7). In this vein, 71% of respondents asserted in the survey that "rather than expecting a great improvement in school performance test scores, [they] concentrate on individual students' growth, no matter how small." Few items in the questionnaire found such high approval among teachers from the 11 probationary schools.

When asked what were "[their] expectations for the school to improve noticeably in the near future," survey respondents were divided. Roughly half (Kentucky, 45%; Maryland, 60%) were certain of such improvements.

But success was not necessarily framed by test scores, as for this second-grade teacher from Kentucky who asserted that "things are going to improve" but didn't "know about scores" (10-5) in this regard, or the teacher who felt that despite improvement gains, the school was always "one step behind" the system's expectations (40-04; sixth-grade reading teacher). While more optimistic about incremental improvements, reaching official standards drew more pessimism:

> I'm always an optimist, yeah, I think it's [probation] going to be taken off. . . . But anytime soon? No! (G-17; mathematics teacher).

> Well, it is not impossible. I wouldn't say that it is impossible, but I wouldn't say that it's highly likely. (B-6; sixth-grade social studies teacher)

> In our time? [Laughs] Oh, Lord. Not without some real radical revolutionary change, I don't think so. (D-3)

Teachers from the four Kentucky schools were more pessimistic about their school's prospects and the realism of the state's goals than the Maryland respondents. Judging from the interviews, this pessimism can be attributed to a greater doubt among the sampled Kentucky teachers about their efficacy with difficult students and the sense in two of the four schools that they had become their district's dumping ground for weak students. An eighth-grade English teacher expressed the sentiment of some of her colleagues:

> I say this and I mean this seriously, they can do whatever they want and bring as many different faculty members in here and experts and everything, but they're not going to change this school until they change the student population, until we get more role models in this school. (40-02)

A particular Maryland feature was teachers' uncertainty of how to "get off the list." At the time the interviews were conducted, no school had ever exited probation in that state:

> I'm glad you're using a pseudonym for me, because the reason I don't think this school's successful is because . . . I'm always observant and always read, and always listen to, news, and I don't know any place that's been successful. So, why do I expect it to be successful at [School C]? I never knew of any place so far that reconstitution, that there's been a success rate. (C-2; guidance counselor)

Widespread skepticism notwithstanding, optimism was an act of faith, the only option in this situation for many:

So I have to be optimistic enough to say that this is all going to work out. . . . That's a strong statement. Because I have no choice. (A-16; English department head)

I really believe we can change, and that's the bottom line. We're just going to do it. . . . I'm, I *am* optimistic. I *do* love . . . these kids. (A-3; reading specialist)

There's only one way to go. We can't get worse. (C-11; first-grade teacher)

I believe, I believe it will be. I can *see* the difference already. (F-6)

Yes. Anything is possible. (F-9)

I have to trust that they [the test scores] will be [higher], you know, because if I don't have faith, I'm not going to perform. (G-11; seventh/eighth-grade mathematics teacher)

A less faith-based and more reasoned optimism linked performance hopes for improvements to the new funds the schools received, new personnel the school had on board, and new instructional programs the districts had acquired. Hope was often conditioned on the availability of these additional resources:

So yes, I do think we can improve, given, but with the notation that only given what we ask for. (A-2, eighth-grade science teacher)

I feel very confident that with the help that we are going to get. . . . We've set standards and goals. . . . The additional materials that we need, hopefully additional staff people that we need, different clubs and things that will be in the making. . . . I feel very positive that all of this is going to help our scores to improve. And more staff development for the teachers. (C-4; media specialist)

Principals especially stressed that additional resources were indispensible if the school was to make progress:

The superintendent told me when he hired me that he wasn't pleased with the academic performance of the school. I can make a difference. Give me what I need, and I can make a difference. (A-1; middle school principal)

Well, I feel confident that I have done the job that I can do to make a difference in the school, but the test data shows different. However, I feel that if I get the resources, the human resources, physical resources as well as the budget that I need, I can turn this school around totally. The vision that I have set forth for myself is a school of excellence. I believe that we can reach that. (C-1; elementary school principal)

In schools that experienced test score increases in years prior to the decline that led to probation, some teachers voiced confidence that past performance might be repeated, and a few teachers based their optimism on improvements they had already sensed since the school had become probationary, such as improved discipline. But for the most part, optimism was only infrequently linked to classroom changes. A minority of teachers stated that they simply worked harder, and in a few instances teachers pointed to the visibly beneficial effects of new programs in their classrooms. In elementary schools, new phonics-based reading programs, such as Open Court or Success for All, instilled hope.

Only a few teachers mentioned high expectations for students as a prerequisite for success, such as a seventh-grade English teacher who constantly reminded herself not to lower her standards:

To keep my standards high and to make sure that they know what I expect of them and what this school and this county expect of them. But sometimes you get, when you see a whole class that doesn't meet the standards, you want to lower your standards, and you just have to somehow pull it out of them. (B-15; seventh-grade English teacher)

Administrators and teachers with special assignments, such as instructional specialists or DE/HSEs, had a different perspective. In interviews with them, instructional changes were either the main reasons for optimism or the main condition on which their optimism hinged:

I think teachers have now come to grips with the fact that the old stand up and lecture type instruction is no longer apropos to students of today. . . . I think probably the biggest thing that will take us there is the change that teachers are incurring in instructional methodology. (G-7; assistant principal)

But even the most committed and skillful instructional specialists voiced doubt, such as the instructional coordinator at School B who gave a rather sophisticated analysis compared to the rest of the interviewees and deserves to be quoted at length:

> I look at it more with the test. What is the problem with the test? Because, actually, when I step out and look at what the county is doing as a whole, for example, _____ School is the number one middle school right now. Their composite index is the highest in the county; they're at 26. That is a school that literally handpicks who comes to them. I mean, there is a very strict criteria—you either meet it or you don't. So they are taking the cream of the cream of the crop from the entire county. Their composite index is 18 points higher than ours in this building. With, obviously, we don't have a criteria, we get whoever comes to our door, and it's ever-changing. So when you look at it that way, they are operating 18 points higher than we are, again not meeting the state standard. I have to really start taking a look at the tests and seeing, I mean . . . if we are saying these are the brightest and these are the best and they are not meeting a state standard, I think people are very confused about what exactly that standard should be or is. . . . I believe in the premise of the test, which is to have a child that can think critically and write well. So the premise of the test is good. What I think is that for this age group of kids, it is not realistic to not take into account the differing popula-tions when you are 12 years old or 13 years old. And the test is just not willing to make any accommodations for social backgrounds, ethnic backgrounds, that kind of things. It's just a very, very real problem. . . . I would say in general, no [the school will not reach the state's goal]. I mean, every year, we have a few kids who do well on the test. Last year we had quite a few kids do well on the test. But for the most part, it puts them in situations or gives them reading material that is so foreign to them. (B-20)

It was a recurring theme that the chances for improving performance depended on faculty cohesion, unity, and stability; harmonious and support-ive relationships between faculty and administration; and collective effort—"everyone kind of picking up their bootstraps and doing their very best that he or she can do" (C-3; science department chair). But effort alone could not get the job done unless more quality teachers were supplied to the schools:

> The only way these scores are going to improve is if they hire edu-cated teachers, which they're not doing. So, I don't . . . , good luck to

them. I don't see how they're going to do it. . . . I wish them the best of luck, but I think it's going to be very difficult, and I almost think that the kids are getting more pressure about it than the teachers are because a lot of the teachers really just don't care. So, the students are taking the brunt of it. (D-21; sixth-grade mathematics teacher)

In summary, a large majority of respondents expressed doubts about their school reaching the official standards. Respondents were more hopeful for incremental improvements in their schools. Optimism was guarded and mixed with doubt. For many teachers, optimism was an article of faith or was based on factors outside of their control, such as additional resources, personnel, programs, and so on. Expectations of success were often coupled with expectations for more help. Judging from the interviews, probation per se did not necessarily make teachers more pessimistic as long it was seen as supportive rather than punitive.

A number of teachers acknowledged the necessity for increased effort, but these demands were not personalized. On the whole, teachers in the 11 schools were skeptical as to their chances of exiting probation. There is little evidence that teachers changed their own expectations for students in alignment with the states' expectations. This is understandable given the low validity and fairness teachers attributed to the accountability system.

CHAPTER 3

Motivation and Commitment

WITH MASAKO NISHIO

WE SAW IN THE PREVIOUS two chapters that the majority of teachers across the 11 schools responded to the pressures of probation with ambivalence. In some, sanctions instilled shock and anxiety, at least initially, and most wanted to get rid of the low-performance label to repair their reputation. But they also reasserted their competence, externalized the schools' performance problems, scoffed at the punitiveness of the label, doubted the possibility of further sanctions, and expected additional help from the state. Commitment to stay in the negatively labeled school was precarious. In the eyes of many, the educational meaning of the accountability system was low. Although they were generally willing to be directed by the system, they also saw it as largely invalid, unfair, and unrealistic in the context of their schools. Only a minority, often teachers in leadership roles, saw the system as sound and probation as good pressure. Prevalent sentiments among teachers in the 11 schools paint a picture of probation as a somewhat muted force for school improvement.

In this chapter we shift the analytical angle. We want to better understand why some teachers are more motivated by probation and are more apt to maintain their commitment to the negatively labeled schools than are others. To this end, we compare groups with reportedly different work motivation and commitment levels and try to discern factors that could explain these differences.

One could imagine that teachers who feel particularly anxious about probation pressures and who are prone to be directed by the accountability system are especially motivated to increase work effort. But these very same teachers could also be the ones who, trying to dodge an anxiety-producing situation, have low commitment to stay.

If the policy worked properly, we would also expect teachers for whom the accountability system is meaningful—that is, who believe in the validity, fairness, and realism of the system—to be more highly motivated and at the same time more strongly committed to the improvement of their school.

Moving from systemic factors to more up-close ones, we already saw that being an administrator or instructional specialist changes one's perspective on accountability. But other factors may come into play. We could imagine that teachers who perceive their work environment as supportive and capable of meeting the challenge and who perceive themselves as especially competent would be both more motivated and more committed to stay. In this chapter, we pursue these hypotheses and conclude the analysis of teacher motivation under probation.

LEVELS OF ENGAGEMENT AND WORK EFFORT

We use two indicators of motivation here: reported engagement in school improvement activities and reported level of work effort as a result of probation. Engagement in improvement is defined as a combination of involvement in school improvement activities and the perceived effect of probation on one's work. By cross-tabulating the variables "involvement in school improvement activities" and "job effects of probation," we created three groups of teachers with different engagement levels: One group was highly involved in school improvement activities and highly affected in their work by probation, a second group was somewhat involved and affected, and a third group was fairly uninvolved and only weakly affected. The proportion of those who were highly involved and affected—that is, those who were most intensely reached by probation—was about 25%.

Likewise, by cross-tabulating the variables "working harder due to probation" and "increased work hours due to probation," we created three groups of teachers. We defined these three groups as having exerted strong, moderate, and little effort due to probation. A plurality of respondents (45%) indicated that they had exerted strong effort. Only about 15% of the sample reported little effort. One needs to keep in mind, however, that many teachers who responded to the survey tended to be teacher activists.

Our two indicators of motivation, engagement and effort, are not necessarily similar and are treated here as two separate constructs, both desirable for school improvement. Engagement refers to involvement in distinct improvement activities that have had an effect on one's work. These activities need not require an increase in work hours if one merely shifted one's activity focus to probation-related activities. Effort, on the other hand, is a very generic and at times subtle behavior that can occur schoolwide or in individual teachers' work spheres. The correlation between involvement in activities and increased work hours for our sample is .20 (significant at the .01 level).

Engagement

Analysis of variance (see Table 3.1) reveals that teachers with higher levels of engagement responded to pressure with more career anxiety and a stronger sense of being directed. Differences for direction are particularly strong between modestly and highly engaged groups. Goal importance—defined as the desire to increase test scores and get rid of the probation label—was stronger for higher levels of engagement as well. By contrast, sense of meaningfulness—defined as belief in the validity, fairness, and realism of the accountability system—was

Table 3.1. Factors Associated with Levels of Engagement in Probation (ANOVA)

| | Mean | | | |
	Least Engaged [a]	Moderately Engaged [b]	Strongly Engaged [c]	F
Commitment	−.49	−.02	.12	2.26
Pressure				
Career anxiety	−.70	.08	.04	4.946**
Direction	−.13	−.16	.59	12.28***
Meaning				
Goal importance	−.80	−.08	.30	8.47***
Validity	.13	−.02	−.03	.20
(Un)fairness	.21	−.05	.22	1.51
(Un)realism	.22	.05	−.15	1.03
Expectation of improvement	−.73	−.01	.08	4.62*
Competence				
Skills of self	−.05	−.08	.35	3.86*
Efficacy	−.16	−.15	.32	4.02*
Professionalism	−.05	−.06	.33	3.17*
Organizational capacity				
Skills of colleagues	−.41	−.01	.20	2.45
Collegiality	−.76	.08	.17	5.96**
Principal support	−.55	.07	.12	3.16*
Principal control	−1.02	−.02	.36	12.44***

[a] $N = 18$ (8.3%).

[b] $N = 146$ (67.0%).

[c] $N = 54$ (24.8%).

*$p < .05$. **$p < .01$. ***$p < .001$.

not different for the three engagement levels. Only expectation of success, thought of as system-unspecific incremental improvement, made a difference.

On the level of individual competence (professionalism, efficacy, skills of self), differences were significant between the highly and moderately engaged. On the organizational level (collegiality, leadership), differences were strong among all three levels, most strongly in teachers' perceptions of their principal as controlling.

Thus, differences between the highly engaged and less engaged were particularly strong with regard to the importance of external performance goals, direction, and principal control. (The statistical procedure used here does not allow for an analysis of effects of one variable controlled for all others.) A combination of external and internal pressures and directions may have loomed large in teachers' decision to become engaged. Being indifferent to the system's meaningfulness and confident of one's competence in the face of the low-performance label while simultaneously responding to external pressure and feeling controlled by the principal makes for a distinctly externally driven engagement dynamic. In all likelihood, this hierarchical pattern was more pronounced in the Maryland schools, where the proportion of educators perceiving their faculties as collegial was smaller and the proportion perceiving their principals as controlling was larger. But there were no statistically significant differences with regard to engagement between respondents from the two states.

Across both states, probation affected senior teachers more strongly. The difference in work experience between the least and most engaged groups was an average of 7 years. The strongly engaged group had worked on the average almost twice as long in the educational system as the least engaged (not displayed in Table 3.1). By contrast, length of tenure at the school was not significantly different for engagement levels.

Confirming the picture we laid out in the previous two chapters, only a relatively small proportion of respondents was highly engaged. Those more highly engaged individuals felt external pressure more acutely as career anxiety, were more directed, and wanted to be rid of the label. Interestingly, contradicting our initial theories of action about probation, the more engaged did not embrace the accountability system as more meaningful. Not surprisingly, and predicted by those who claim internalized meanings as prerequisites of commitment to one's work, the more highly engaged under these circumstances were not necessarily more committed to stay in the difficult work environment, a serious problem for school improvement.

Work Effort

Although engagement and effort capture different types of behavior, the overall pattern is similar for both (see Table 3.2), but clearly more pronounced

Table 3.2. Factors Associated with Levels of Work Effort Due to Probation (ANOVA)

	Mean			
	Exerted Little Effort [a]	Exerted Moderate Effort [b]	Exerted Strong Effort [c]	F
Commitment	−.12	.02	.04	.32
Pressure				
Career anxiety	−.65	−.11	.33	17.04**
Direction	−.25	−.16	.18	4.60*
Meaning				
Goal importance	−.20	−.03	.06	1.00
Validity	.06	.11	−.17	2.24
(Un)fairness	−.24	−.19	.28	7.14**
(Un)realism	−.24	−.15	.23	5.21**
Expectation of success	−.36	.11	−.03	2.98
Competence				
Skills of self	−.20	−.09	.11	1.76
Efficacy	.04	.09	−.12	1.15
Professionalism	−.06	.01	.03	.12
Organizational capacity				
Skills of colleagues	−.58	−.14	.28	12.59***
Collegiality	−.98	−.07	.37	29.34***
Principal support	−.59	−.003	.14	6.76**
Principal control	−.66	.03	.14	8.70***

[a] $N = 39$ (14.7%).

[b] $N = 106$ (40.0%).

[c] $N = 120$ (45.3%).

*$p < .05$. **$p < .01$. ***$p < .001$.

for levels of effort. What moved teachers to increase effort? Clearly, pressures in the form of career anxiety played a key role and, to a lesser degree, directions given by the system. Teachers did not increase their work effort because they more strongly believed in the meaningfulness of the accountability system. Quite the opposite: Those who exerted strong effort did not attach more importance to the goals of raising test scores and exiting probation. Most noteworthy, they were significantly stronger skeptics regarding the fairness and realism of the accountability system relative to the groups exerting less effort.

If meaningfulness of the accountability system was not a factor inducing higher work effort, conditions in the up-close environment of teachers were. As for engagement, collegial relationships and the perception of colleagues as skillful were key components in teachers' levels of effort (see Table 3.2), as was seniority. The difference between the lowest and the highest effort level was an average of almost 4 years (significant at the .05 level). Again, as for engagement, high effort was not associated with more commitment to stay at the labeled school. Thus, it seems that a combination of external pressure and internal group capacities may have moved educators across the 11 schools to exert more effort. The accountability system, by contrast, seems to have run into a serious "meaning deficit."

LEVELS OF COMMITMENT TO STAY

We saw above that more motivated teachers (i.e., those who were more engaged and exerted more effort) were not necessarily also more committed to stay in the negatively labeled school. This could be a grave problem for probation policies because if teachers who are activated by the policy are just as likely to leave as those who remain unmotivated, then the continuity of any kind of improvement process is imperiled. In fact, this was the situation we encountered in a number of schools. We surmised earlier that it might be the meaning deficit of the accountability system that was responsible for this lack of commitment.

Our analysis (displayed in Table 3.3) suggests as much. The pattern for commitment to stay differs from the patterns for engagement and effort in two main respects: Highly committed teachers believed more strongly in the meaningfulness of the accountability system and at the same time felt no more pressure than less committed respondents. As Table 3.3 shows, higher levels of commitment were associated with higher means on the fairness and realism scales (see Appendix) and only slight or no differences on the direction and career anxiety scales. This finding bolsters the importance of the meaningfulness of the accountability system for a more lasting engagement in school improvement.

Similar to work effort and engagement, teachers' close-up work situation was also important for high commitment, particularly indicated by the higher means for expectation of school improvement and principal support as well as for collegiality and perceived skills of colleagues. By contrast, sense of individual competence did not differ according to commitment level in our sample, which reverberates with findings from the interviews that teachers in all kinds of positions were inclined to leave. As for work engagement and effort, more committed teachers tended to have greater seniority. In our

Table 3.3. Factors Associated with Levels of Commitment to Stay (ANOVA)

	Mean			
	Not Committed [a]	Weakly Committed or Undecided [b]	Strongly Committed [c]	F
Pressure				
Career anxiety	−.03	.04	.02	.096
Direction	−.21	−.23	.15	4.09*
Meaning				
Goal importance	−.31	−.12	.15	4.92**
Validity	−.14	−.08	.05	.96
(Un)fairness	.31	.05	−.17	5.25**
(Un)realism	.34	−.05	−.10	4.55*
Expectation of improvement	−.57	.18	.37	25.47***
Competence				
Skills of self	−.08	−.24	.11	2.52
Efficacy	−.23	−.08	.10	2.44
Professionalism	−.08	−.19	.11	2.08
Organizational capacity				
Skills of colleagues	−.31	−.15	.29	9.67***
Collegiality	−.30	−.17	.28	9.14***
Principal support	−.54	−.06	.32	18.48***
Principal control	−.36	.02	.20	7.29**

[a] $N = 73$ (27.5%).

[b] $N = 57$ (21.5%).

[c] $N = 135$ (50.95%).

*$p < .05$. **$p < .01$. ***$p < .001$.

11-school sample, the mean difference between the least and most committed groups is 4 years of work experience (statistically significant at the .05 level).

PROFILE OF MOTIVATED AND COMMITTED TEACHERS

We can now construct a profile of teachers who are likely to react to probation favorably and increase their level of engagement and effort. As compared to less motivated colleagues, such teachers are further advanced in their careers and are often in a leadership position in their schools. They increase their effort and engagement not because they value the goals and standards of the accountability system or strongly expect to reap rewards but because they feel apprehensive about sanctions, though they discard their seriousness. They are concerned about their public reputation as professionals and motivated by positive characteristics of their work groups. They accept directions, though with ambivalence. Their relatively high levels of work motivation, however, are not associated with a higher commitment to their schools on probation. They probably waver between reaffirming their commitment to their schools and contemplating exit.

But when their belief in the fairness of the label and in the realism and attainability of their goal of exiting probation is high, they are likely to stay at their schools despite the negative performance label. Their career anxiety, on the other hand, is not any higher than that of their less committed colleagues.

This profile speaks to a conundrum of probation in the 11 schools: The policy rouses teachers into action through pressure while at the same time activating a deep skepticism about the system's rightfulness. Longer-term engagement in the face of the negative label, however, seems to thrive when teachers feel fairly evaluated and confronted with goals that are realistic for the children in their care. It is conceivable that without remedying the system's meaning deficit, activism may remain short-term or may even result in longer term burnout.

PROBATION AND TEACHER MOTIVATION—A CONCLUSION

Let us recap. In Chapter 1 we saw how probation initially shocked teachers, especially senior teachers. But in time many teachers distanced themselves from the label. Frequently, they reinterpreted probation as a status of need rather than a performance deficit. The possibility of more severe sanctions was denied. A reassertion of competence and professional quality was pervasive. Problems tended to be externalized. Probation was an irritant, and teachers strove to repair their professional reputation. They accepted the need to raise test scores as a fact of life but pursued this goal with ambivalence. Commitment to stay in the negatively labeled school was precarious, but probation did not trigger an automatic exodus. However, it fostered lack of commitment in conjunction with already difficult working conditions and available exit options. This was true for novice teachers as well as teachers in leadership positions at their schools.

In Chapter 2 we saw that the ambivalence with which teachers pursued the accountability goals had to do with their skepticism about the accountability system. Large majorities found the system to be invalid, unfair, and unrealistic. Many teachers' self-concept ran counter to the accountability system designs. They were not data-driven; rather, they personalized. They were not driven by ambitious quantitative growth spurts but, rather, focused on incremental steps of learning. Intellectual and social growth of individual students, needs of the community, and relationships with colleagues, rather than the maximizing of scores, motivated them to put out effort and stay in a difficult work environment.

Many teachers heeded the system, but they did so without conviction. More teachers let themselves be guided by the system and wanted to be rid of probation than committed themselves to the actual performance goals or viewed their own performance through the lens of the system. Likewise, they derived rewards from encounters with students, not from the mechanisms of the accountability system. In the eyes of many, probation proved the point that not too many rewards could be expected from the external environment of the school.

Thus, the accountability systems did not connect to teachers' prevailing sense of responsibility and established cultures of teaching. Teachers had serious misgivings about the accountability system's educational meaningfulness. It is not surprising, then, that an overwhelming majority of respondents in both states criticized the system's status quo. Only 9% agreed that "the accountability system should remain as is."

In all schools, there were those who considered probation to be good pressure. They were a minority. Often they were teachers or administrators in leadership positions who hoped the label would move their colleagues to do things they would not do under normal circumstances. Very little critical reflection on their own performance was evident. Good pressure did not mean, however, that the pressure was perceived as rightful. Those who reported more engagement and effort as a result of probation tended to respond to external pressure with more apprehension; at the same time, however, they were even more critical of the accountability system and the rightfulness of the low-performance label.

Clearly, educators did not act as a result of having internalized the performance criteria and judgments of the system. These beliefs were neither widespread nor stronger among the more activated educators. If anything, the opposite was the case. High activism was associated with more skepticism. Likewise, self-interested motives did not seem to play an important role since expectations of reaping rewards from the system were low. The meaning deficit of the accountability system depressed teachers' long-term commitment to their embattled school. While those with higher commitment to stay also believed more strongly in the fairness and realism of the system, many who did not were apt to burn out after short spurts of activism. As a result, in our visits to schools we frequently encountered teacher leaders and activists who were initially roused by probation. But doubts about the school's prospects in combination with festering resentments about being treated unfairly fostered desires to leave and to be rid of the pressure.

The consistent strength of organizational characteristics for work motivation and commitment, independent of the accountability system's goals, meanings, and rewards, suggests that teachers' response to probation may be more diffusely related to up-close contexts rather than the incentive mechanisms of the accountability system. Strong leadership and a strong faculty were associated with more motivation and sustained commitment. Interview data suggest that meaningful relationships with students and colleagues generated this kind of commitment to improvement, and probation may have challenged and activated this commitment regardless of teachers' grave doubts about the accountability system. So the accountability system was not internalized, but traditional responsibilities and obligations toward students and colleagues were reactivated. It is conceivable that external pressure, internal vigilance of the principal, a small active core group of teachers, and a general sense of togetherness among staff in support of incremental improvement and in defense of the school against a hostile external environment could move schools forward despite widespread rejection of the accountability system as meaningless.

Ironically, then, probation would draw its strength from sources that accountability systems disregard. By design, high-stakes accountability systems make the performance situation "stronger" by putting clearly focused goal maximizing and self-interested calculating in place of diffuse commitments. Yet expectations of rewards (test score gain, exit from probation) were low, and diffuse commitments were the very sources that sustained the more motivated educators. Accountability systems that tap more forcefully into these commitments would be better tools not only to motivate teachers but also to sustain their motivation for the necessary long term. As it stands, probation capitalizes on educators' traditional commitments and perhaps even idealism in a rather twisted way by pushing to action those segments of a faculty that probably least deserve the low-performance label.

Thus, our analysis of teacher motivation and probation suggests that probation as a tool for improving traditionally difficult schools comes up short as a way to impel the majority of teachers to identify their share of the responsibility for student performance and take the initiative in their own fields of influence. The organizational dynamic that unfolds in the schools as a result of these motivational patterns will be examined in the next part. Rather than being the result of incentives reaching individual teachers, it may be more a matter of the school's organizational dynamic whether teachers increase effort, become engaged, and stay committed.

PART II

Probation and Organizational Development

OUR EMPHASIS NOW SHIFTS from individual beliefs and attitudes to social interactions and organizational strategies. School-site characteristics, we saw, shape teachers' motivation and commitment in important ways. In the two accountability systems studied here, whole schools, rather than individuals, are held responsible, and it is the staff as a performance unit that is to master the crisis of the organization. Avoiding the divisiveness of individual merit-pay schemes (Malen, 1999), group accountability may strengthen collegiality and a sense of collective responsibility and may facilitate the development of shared expectations and internal accountability schoolwide (Abelmann et al., 1999).

In the literature on high-performance organizations (Mohrman et al., 1996), the group as accountability unit is usually understood as the basis for rewards or bonuses for good performance rather than as the unit that may have to absorb sanctions and penalties. But the response of work units to sanctions, perhaps involving high personal stakes, may flow from organizational processes that are quite different from those at work in high-performance or high-involvement organizations. Responses to sanctions may be more adequately captured by a line of inquiry that places the failing organization and its crisis in the center.

Probation induces a crisis that may motivate an organization to learn. An organization learns when "change and improvement occur because the individuals and the groups inside the school are able to acquire, analyze, understand and plan around information that arises from the environment and from internal monitoring" (Louis & Kruse, 1998, p. 18). Schools learn from their status of probation when they engage in a process of internalizing performance standards of the accountability system. At minimum, this process entails dialogue about the goals of the accountability system, the school's share of responsibility for shortcomings, collective commitments to improvement goals, and forms of internal management and accountability that facilitate these commitments.

As probation throws schools into crisis, they may unfreeze. Old routines and mental models (Senge, 1990) are up for internal debate and conflict may arise. A conflict-driven scenario of organizational learning is narrated by Bennett and Ferlie (1994): "A crisis moves awkward issues up agendas. . . . We are likely to see continuing pressure from pioneers, the formation of special groups that seek to evangelize the rest of the organization, high energy and commitment levels and a period of organizational plasticity" (p. 11). In the case of schools, dynamic principals and groups of highly involved teachers inside the organization or community pressure groups and change agents external to the organization could provide the ferment in the micropolitics of the school site.

External threat and induced crisis, however, are not automatic triggers of learning (Levine, Rubin, & Wolohojian, 1982). According to Staw's threat-rigidity model (Staw, Lance, & Dutton, 1981), threats from the environment may cause anxiety and stress, leading to restriction in information processing, reliance on well-learned behavior, and surge in drive and energy. If the group believes in the likelihood of success in meeting the new demand from the environment, increased cohesiveness, support for leadership, but also a tendency to uniformity occur. If the group believes in the likelihood of failure, cohesiveness decreases, leadership becomes unstable, and dissension arises (Staw et al., 1981). The organization is then unable to turn itself around, and often leadership is replaced or personnel exit. In this case, probation would have failed. But even organizations successfully responding to external threats tend to reinforce dominant patterns of operation rather than learn new things, according to this model. Newmann and colleagues (1997) make this point when they observe that in their sample of restructuring schools, strong external accountability pressures were a detriment to the development of internal accountability processes.

In Part II, we investigate these dynamics in more detail. To the degree that probation is perceived as a crisis of the organization, schools could respond by becoming more rigid and hierarchical or they could engage in organizational learning. In the former case, the performance crisis would be weathered though administrative control, centralized decision making, and the adoption of external programs that prescribe what and how teachers should teach. In the latter case, we would find teachers communicating about their responsibilities, sharing their expectations, agreeing on procedures of internal accountability, and seeking out remedies for improvement tailored to their needs. The preponderance of one pattern over the other may have serious repercussions for teachers' behavior in the semiautonomous classroom space.

We begin our analysis with a comparison of two sets of schools from the state of Maryland. We present the cases of schools that moved (Rosenholtz, 1991) toward improvement in Chapter 4 and of those that got stuck in decline or low performance in Chapter 5. We show what interactions took place and what improvement strategies were chosen. In Chapter 6, we widen the angle beyond the focal case study schools from Maryland by examining what school improvement plans from a larger number of schools can tell us about the response patterns of schools on probation. We then contrast the Maryland patterns with those found in the Kentucky schools and finally draw conclusions about patterns of organizational development under probation.

CHAPTER 4

Schools Moving Toward Improvement

WITH KIM CURTIS AND LEA PLUT-PREGELJ

WE SELECTED TWO OUT OF THE SEVEN Maryland sites as moving schools because field researchers had identified these two schools, Schools B and C, as highly activist in their response to probation, and survey data independently confirmed that they had higher mean levels of reported engagement and work effort relative to the stuck schools. Schools D and E most strongly contrasted with the two moving schools in this regard. We borrowed the terms "moving " and "stuck" from Rosenholtz (1991). But in the context of our study the terms distinguish between schools that take a more proactive stance toward school improvement in the face of probation and schools in which such a stance is less in evidence. This is indicated by different mean levels of engagement and effort due to probation as measured by the survey and researchers' ratings based on data from the field work. Test score data were not our original criterion to distinguish between moving and stuck schools. But test scores mirror these motivational patterns. Before we delve into the stories of the moving schools, we need to give a brief overview of the conditions and challenges that all Maryland schools faced in order to better understand in context the moving schools' efforts to improve.

THE MARYLAND SCHOOLS

The challenges were similar in the moving and the stuck schools: poverty, organizational instability, and erratic fluctuations in test scores. These conditions shaped personal interactions at school sites and constrained choices of improvement strategies.

Poverty

All seven selected Maryland schools had a distinctly urban character. Three schools, one middle school and two elementary schools, were truly inner-city schools. They were located in the midst of or close to extreme urban poverty and blight, and their populations' poverty indicators were very high. Percentages of students receiving free or reduced-price lunches were 70% and higher. Four schools were located at the edges of large cities. While their physical surroundings were more pleasant, their populations were for the most part bused in from poorer parts of their districts. One of the four, the moving elementary school, had a distinctly inner-city character despite its nominal suburban district locale. The three middle schools, located in the inner suburban ring around the city, were less impacted by poverty, with between 40% and 60% of students qualifying for free or reduced-price lunches. One of these schools is the moving middle school in the sample. All seven schools were attended almost exclusively by African American students.

Though impacted by poverty, the schools did not conform to the stereotype of a neglected urban school, broken and out of control, perhaps with the exception of one inner-city middle school whose dark hallways, menacing hall monitors, loitering students, and vandalized classrooms made it a forbidding place. For the most part, the schools studied had lobbies that were brightened with plants and colorful displays of students' projects, school spirit banners, recognition plaques, and trophies. Many classrooms we visited reflected the instructional program in the display of student work and gave evidence to the personal care teachers expended on creating a friendly environment. Nevertheless, almost all of the schools suffered from structural neglect. Most schools lacked proper ventilation, and many needed basic repairs. Two schools were severely overcrowded. For example, one elementary school, built in the 1960s for 350 students, had an enrollment of 651 students when it was identified as reconstitution-eligible in 1998. Thirteen portable classrooms were added to house the overflow. One middle school, also built in the 1960s as an elementary school, enlarged and renovated in 1973 to house 500 students, had 780 students at the time the school received the low-performance designation. In this school, much instruction took place in a severely overcrowded basement that was arranged as an open-classroom area dating back to its early years as an elementary school. Each school grappled with specific circumstances. Though urban in character and in need of physical repair, six of the seven schools were not unpleasant places thanks to visible efforts on the part of the teachers there.

Organizational Instability

With combined annual entrant and withdrawal rates ranging from between 30% and 60%, student mobility was high in our sample schools. Teachers attributed this transience to high levels of student poverty. High rates of teacher turnover, common across the seven Maryland schools in our sample, exacerbated teachers' inability to provide stable learning environments. On average, annual teacher turnover rates ranged from anywhere between a quarter to half of the staff. Across the seven schools, relatively more experienced teachers were replaced by younger, inexperienced, and often provisionally certified teachers. For example in School E, of the 14 new teachers hired for the 1998–1999 schoolyear, just 2 were certified to teach elementary school. Teacher turnover throughout the period of our study changed the age composition of faculties. More novice teachers entered probationary schools, late-career teachers with more than 15 years of work experience remained, but increasingly midcareer teachers with between 5 and 15 years of experience turned their backs on working in these schools. In general, the majority of the teachers at the seven schools had fewer than 5 years of experience (46% on the survey). An overwhelming 71% of the survey respondents had been at their school for 5 years or less (the comparable figure for the four Kentucky schools was 53%). With so many new and inexperienced staff members arriving each year, the schools were prevented from developing a stable cadre of well-trained professionals capable of providing the type of instruction needed for their students to meet the state's rigorous performance standards.

Chronic administrative turnover was also found in most of the Maryland schools. One middle school had been overseen by no less than eight administrators in the last 15 years. Since many reconstitution-eligible schools (including the seven selected schools) improved only marginally or not at all after identification, punitive transfers of principals were frequent. In four of the seven schools, the low-performance designation was accompanied with an immediate change of the principal. Two of the four new principals did not survive their first year after designation; one was transferred after his second year. One school had a new principal every year for the 3 years of data collection. In three schools, the long-term principals survived the designation, but they felt highly uncertain in their tenure. One of them subsequently lost her job and chose early retirement, leaving only two principals who survived the low-performance designation in their assignments. One of those two retained his job against the explicit wish of the state department to remove him and one retired 2 years after his school's probation designation.

When the turnover of adults in a school becomes rapid and the proportion of those who are in the prime of their careers diminishes from year to year, the notion of a school on probation that assumes responsibility for past performance deficiencies and strives to improve over a period of several years becomes obsolete because there is little continuity on which the school improvement processes can be built. We saw earlier that more senior teachers responded to probation more strongly and retained their commitment to the school (while at the same time being also more skeptical). Thus, increasing numbers of novices will in all likelihood weaken the motivational impact of probation and the resolve to stay at the school despite the negative label. The high teacher turnover puts in doubt the rationale for group accountability and for an assessment system that charts progress by measuring year-to-year performance snapshots for the school as a whole.

Test Score Fluctuations

In general, probationary status had a positive, albeit small, effect on these troubled and declining schools in the area of MSPAP achievement (see Figures 4.1 and 4.2), the most weighty component in the state's school performance assessments. Formulated in a positive way, in the post-identification period the seven schools were generally able to score at least as well as they did on the year's test that made them reconstitution-eligible. That is, they did not decline further. However, improvements were very modest, except in a few cases. In this respect, our sample of seven schools resembles the test score development of a larger number of schools on probation in Maryland.

Whether MSPAP or MFT scores are adequate measures of a school's performance from year to year is not our concern here. While we do not intend to causally explain the schools' performance on the state assessments, we use test scores as one important data point that contributes to our understanding of what schools do under conditions of probation. Our analysis is challenged to do two things: to understand the overall flat performance of the seven schools that resembles the performance of the majority of schools on probation in Maryland, and to identify those conditions and responses that coincide with performance improvement.

As for the moving schools, looking at MSPAP reading and math scores (see Figures 4.1 and 4.2)—the areas where almost all schools put their improvement emphasis—we see that the moving Schools B and C gained overall while the stuck Schools D and E either declined or remained fairly stagnant during the time of the study (1998–2000). But both moving schools also started out higher; that is, they had higher test scores at the inception of the current accountability system in 1993 than the other five schools.

But there are important exceptions to this general trend. Like reconstitution-eligible schools in Maryland on the whole, the selected schools experienced inconsistencies across subjects and fluctuations from year to year, rather than continuous trends. For example, in the 3-year period from 1998 to 2000, the moving School C's math scores fluctuated from 7.5% to 25% to 15.8% of students scoring "satisfactory" on the state's MSPAP test, and the stuck School E's math scores during the same period surged from 16.1% to 21.7% until it finally settled on 2% "satisfactory." Thus, the moving schools were not consistently improving their test scores, and the stuck schools

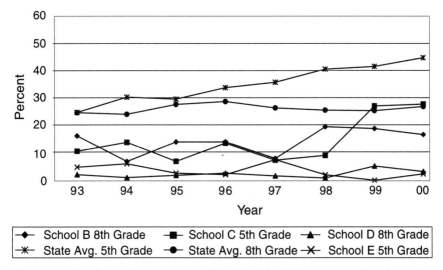

Figure 4.1. Reading performance on MSPAP by school: Percentage of students obtaining satisfactory scores, 1993–2000.

may have seen test score improvements in the past or in parts of their performance.

Motivation and Commitment—Moving and Stuck Schools Compared

Similar to the analysis of differential levels of motivation and commitment (Chapter 3), we conducted a comparison of moving and stuck schools that showed us differences in the way survey respondents perceived the pressures of probation, the meaningfulness of the accountability system, individual competence, and school capacities (see Table 4.1). Educators in the moving schools felt on the whole more directed, though not more anxious, and they attached greater importance to raising test scores. But the accountability system was not more meaningful for them. Means for realism and fairness were not significantly higher, and means for validity were actually lower. By contrast, organizational capacity in the moving schools was higher, particularly means for perceived skills of colleagues, collegiality, and principal support. Similar to high individual engagement and effort, in the moving schools educators in the aggregate were not more committed than in the stuck schools. In fact, commitment was even lower in the moving schools, but the difference was not statistically significant.

Thus, the comparison between moving and stuck schools shows that in the moving schools internalization of the accountability goals as meaning-

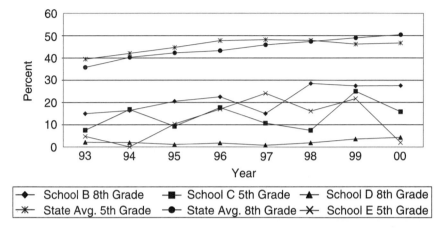

Figure 4.2. Math performance on MSPAP by school: Percentage of students obtaining satisfactory scores, 1993–2000.

ful and commitment to stay were, if anything, even more problematic than in the stuck schools. But organizational capacity was the key internal source of motivation that was clearly more in evidence in the moving schools according to teachers' perceptions. But again, higher willingness to become engaged and exert effort did not necessarily translate into doing so for the longer term.

The Challenge

Poverty, a high number of students at risk from traditionally underprivileged African American backgrounds, a rampant instability of social relationships due to high teacher and student turnover, and a stubborn stagnancy or erratic fluctuation of test scores—these are the challenges that schools had to reckon with when crafting a response to probation. These challenges were coupled with teachers' skepticism toward the accountability system. With the exception of a minority of teachers, mainly specialists outside the classroom, principals could not build on a groundswell of mobilization and self-initiative that probation and high stakes accountability could have, in theory, unleashed. In addition, commitment to stay at the labeled school was precarious. This motivational pattern was prevalent in both the moving and the stuck schools. In the moving schools teachers' attitudes toward the system were perhaps even more negative and their attitudes toward their schools, clearly more positive.

For principals, on the other hand, probation involved high stakes and created a crisis for their organizations. Principals knew that their jobs were

Table 4.1. Comparison of Moving and Stuck Schools (independent samples *t* test)

| | Mean (standardized) | | |
	Moving Schools [a]	Stuck Schools [b]	*t*
Commitment	−.39	−.05	−1.59
Engagement	.17	−.47	2.72**
Effort	.13	−.60	3.94***
Pressure			
Career anxiety	.05	−.15	1.08
Direction	.30	−.39	3.16**
Meaning			
Goal importance	.28	−.15	2.10*
Validity	−.33	.18	−2.35*
(Un)fairness	−.05	−.26	.93
(Un)realism	−.11	−.15	.19
Expectation of improvement	.17	−.25	2.01*
Competence			
Skills of self	.40	−.25	3.06**
Efficacy	.29	.07	1.19
Professionalism	.07	.15	−.36
Organizational capacity			
Skills of colleagues	.05	−.71	3.75***
Collegiality	−.04	−.71	3.26**
Principal support	.12	−.37	2.26*
Principal control	.09	−.30	1.80

[a] $N = 44$.

[b] $N = 58$.

*$p < .05$. **$p < .01$. ***$p < .001$.

tied to test score improvement. However, the principals' commitment and determination were tempered by three factors. First, not unlike many teachers, principals felt buffeted by the ups and downs of test scores rather than in control of them. Even in schools that posted gains, principals were not sure which strategies, out of all the ones they had tried, were actually the ones that caused success. Second, the principals were aware of the districts' inclination to move them swiftly when short-term test score gains were not forthcoming. Hence, they calculated their chances of success with a tone of resignation. Third, districts customarily rotate principals for a variety of reasons regardless of the school's performance scores, making transfers less punitive and more a fact of life for principals. Nevertheless, more than any other actor at the school site, it was the principal who felt the pressure of accountability.

While in theory the accountability system holds whole organizations accountable for performance and is geared to provide incentives for individual teachers to improve instruction, in actuality it targets the principal as the sole responsible actor who is made to stand for the performance of the organization and vicariously experiences the imposition of sanctions that personally hurt. High-stakes school accountability in the Maryland system was in essence high-stakes principal accountability, and thus the schools' response to probation was primarily a matter of leadership.

In fact, whereas the motivational thrust of the accountability system via systemic mechanisms may have been as blunt in the moving schools as in the stuck schools, leadership in combination with organizational capacity and external support made a difference in the moving schools and led to higher levels of teacher engagement and work effort. How this dynamic plays out at the two moving schools in our selection is described next.

SCHOOL B—A MOVING MIDDLE SCHOOL

School B was the moving middle school in the sample. Despite its low-performance label, School B was in a more fortunate situation than many other Maryland schools on probation. Of the middle schools in the sample, it scored highest on the MSPAP from the inception of the accountability system. With a student mobility rate of approximately 30% and just 40% of the school population qualifying for free or reduced-price lunches, the school was less impacted by poverty. Its surroundings, a fairly solid neighborhood, bolstered its image. It was located in a district that had relatively few schools on probation, so the school was supported with an additional $150,000 to its regular budget. The school had a magnet program and even though a recent state auditing team could not detect a curricular differentiation between the magnet and the regular programs, teachers in the school thought the program was useful in attracting better students.

The school was identified as reconstitution-eligible in January of 1998 when its 1996–1997 MSPAP composite index plummeted by more than 9 points. Hence, at the time of data collection, the low-performance label was fresh. Prior to this drop, the school had been making relatively steady progress on both its MSPAP and MSF test results. According to those at School B, the severity of the decline, as opposed to a persistent pattern of low performance, was the reason the school was added to the state's probationary list. As dramatic as the 1997 test score decline was for School B, its rebound the following year proved to be even more dramatic, though in subsequent years test scores either stagnated or even dipped a little. Staff members were at a loss to explain these fluctuations. Given consistency in improvement strategies, teachers mentioned the mindset of student cohorts from year to year and teacher turnover.

Although turnover was high, School B had been able to maintain a level of stability that was higher compared to other schools on probation. Exemplifying this stability is the fact that the principal had been at the school for 18 years, an increasingly rare situation in a school district that had experienced a principal turnover rate of over 40% in the study period. 1997 marked a turning point for School B, when it lost half of its eighth-grade teaching staff, a key testing grade for the state test.

Approximately 50% of the core teaching staff working at School B during the 1999–2000 schoolyear had arrived in the years since it was placed on probation in 1998. Hence, they were not around when the school declined. In particular, the math and science departments were especially hard hit, with 8 of the 10 teachers in each of these departments either in their first or second year of teaching at School B. During interviews, members of both the administration and teaching staff commented on an unusually large turnover after the 1998–1999 schoolyear, School B's first full year as a probation school. While the majority of teachers interviewed said they enjoyed working with the faculty and staff at School B and noted that they would not leave for a school with similar characteristics, many remarked that they had either seriously considered or would consider taking opportunities elsewhere.

Leadership and Interactions

Relating to School B's faculty and staff in a paternalistic way, the principal possessed a quiet, steady demeanor. He was generally described by teachers as easily approachable, willing to listen, and responsive to their needs. According to teachers, while he tried to use a consensual approach when making decisions, he always had the last say. Reflecting findings from interviews, 72% of surveyed teachers viewed the principal as "supportive and encouraging" and 69% characterized him as being responsible for setting priorities, making plans, and seeing that they were carried out. His leadership style was generally top-down, but also caring.

Although he was low-key by nature, many teachers who had been at the school for a number of years noted a striking change in the principal's intensity level once the school had been identified as low-performing. The principal himself noted that he took the news very personally and felt as though he had "failed" as an educator. Pressure from the state department to have him removed made it clear to him that his future as principal of School B hinged on MSPAP improvement. Thus, he made it his overriding concern to raise test scores at the school. From the very beginning, he tried to keep his staff informed about "what was coming down the road" and sought to reinforce the "advantages" of the school's new status—namely, that the school would receive additional funds and assistance. He communicated to teachers and parents that he saw no sense in "fighting" the situation. At the same time, he asked for their assistance in moving forward to implement the school improvement procedures that had been laid out by the state.

Teachers reported that probation made the principal much more interested in what was going on inside their classrooms. In fact, a full 89% of teachers surveyed found that, as a result of reconstitution eligibility, they received more attention from the administration. The principal made weekly visits to classrooms to observe lessons and ensure compliance with school reform measures. During these visits he evaluated teachers' performance using a checklist system. Those found to be not in compliance received memos in their boxes the next day. Having previously enjoyed a relatively high level of autonomy within the classroom, teachers found the new intrusive policies to be stressful. A feeling prevailed that "it's like everything is MSPAP. We're being watched" (B4).

At the same time, the principal also authorized his administrative support staff, including the instructional coordinator, the master teacher, and the school improvement resource teacher (SIRT), to be a very visible presence in teachers' classrooms. In response to the pressures of probation and with the help of new probation-related funds, the principal had recruited some of his most capable teachers into these new positions. Highly skilled and generally well regarded, these teachers were responsible for the majority of the day-to-day teacher–administrator interactions that occurred at School B. They were frequently found observing classrooms, meeting with teachers, and providing in-service training opportunities. But they also oversaw the day-to-day implementation of improvement measures enumerated in the school improvement plan (SIP). For example, they co-chaired weekly team meetings with the principal and reviewed faculty lesson plans for alignment with the SIP. While the instructional coordinator bemoaned this "negative way to operate" (B-20), she believed that without the administration's follow-up, the SIP's school improvement measures would languish.

But this new oversight role was delicate, and it brought with it the disadvantage that, in the words of one of them, she "had been a teacher the year before and here [she] comes back in August and suddenly can come in and say: 'So what's going on in here.'" (B-20). The teachers understood that the principal backed up his new leadership team, but tact, a nonthreatening demeanor, cheerful disposition, and visible skill on the part of the instructional specialists eased their transition into a supervisory role.

Not all teachers were open to heightened scrutiny at the hands of their former peers. For example, one science teacher specifically said that she was initially upset when she found out that "someone from the English department" was "grading" her lesson plan and making suggestions about her content. Indeed, many teachers privately grumbled about their need to comply with numerous administrative mandates. However, although this grumbling was at times loud, compliance appeared to be relatively high. One teacher of unusually long standing attributed the high level of teacher conformity to School B's large number of new teachers so that there was "nobody to oppose [the principal]" (B-4). She believed that if the building had been filled with more experienced teachers, he wouldn't have been able to push through so many changes so quickly. Indeed, the open conflict between the administration and faculty members that led to the departure of many highly experienced teachers during the school's first post-probationary year serves to confirm this sentiment.

Interestingly, while several of School B's teachers expressed disdain for many of the new measures implemented by the principal and his administrative team, most did not express dislike for the principal himself. In fact, a striking number of teachers commented that the principal had played a large role in their decision to stay on at School B despite their various grievances, most notably the high level of stress brought on by heightened teacher accountability. The principal proved adept at deflecting responsibility for the numerous interventions and teacher accountability measures instituted at the school since it had been named reconstitution-eligible. He succeeded in diffusing teacher ire by playing the role of the reluctant enforcer. As one teacher noted, the state "is putting a huge amount of pressure on him and he in turn puts huge amounts of pressure on the teachers" (B-4).

Once on probation, the principal began to conduct weekly meetings with the various grade-level teams that divided into magnet and nonmagnet subdivisions. These weekly team meetings, conducted in the principal's rather cramped office, were the only faculty meetings that regularly took place at School B. Assemblies of the whole faculty were discontinued. While the leadership team viewed these meetings as mini in-service opportunities where teachers were given tips and strategies for improving student performance on MSPAP-related tasks, teachers perceived their function at least in part as a means to "check up" on their performance:

> During weekly team meetings, if you haven't . . . if you've dropped the ball, he will let you know. He doesn't call you out individually, but within the group he will emphasize more. . . . Lets you know specifically, you dropped the ball. (B-12)

That the meetings were conducted in the principal's office only reinforced their accountability bent to the teachers. In almost all of the observed team meetings, either the principal or a member of the leadership team presented the tasks for the week, leaving it to the teachers to ask questions of clarification or make suggestions for implementation.

Outside of these team meetings, collegial interaction occurred in informal channels, though many teachers perceived their faculty as unified and supportive. The team structure impeded significant cross-team interactions in the building, and opportunities to come together in formal meetings without control of the leadership team were few. Many teachers commented that they were generally unfamiliar with the methods and practices of other teams. Some teachers reported feeling isolated by School B's team emphasis, and others expressed a desire for more regular content-area interactions. However, most seemed to accept their limited peer interactions as unproblematic. Undoubtedly, teachers' willingness to forgo additional faculty exchanges stemmed from their fervent desire to keep meetings to an absolute minimum, lest they impinge on scarce planning time that was already taken up in large part by meetings with the principal and student and parent conferences.

According to teachers, discussions concerning curricular issues or instructional strategies were not common occurrences outside the weekly team meetings. Apart from instructions received from administrators, instructional specialists, and external consultants, teachers made no mention of instances in which they were asked to share their expertise with their colleagues in any systematic manner. Nor were there any discussions about the goals and wisdom of the accountability system. Some teachers bemoaned this lack of meaningful opportunity for formal collegial interactions:

> Something that I would like to see implemented would be more
> collaboration among the teachers, in a, in sort of a cross-curriculum
> way, sharing of ideas mainly to observe one another. I mean, I think
> if we could have more interaction, other than casual passing through,
> that that could possibly help to build us . . . because there are some
> very strong, experienced teachers and a lot of times teachers just
> don't get an opportunity to talk to their colleagues about what
> they're doing and see, and actually see, how they do it. (B-13)

Strategies for Improvement

Once being named reconstitution-eligible, School B implemented several wide-ranging strategies aimed specifically at improving MSPAP performance. An in-depth analysis of MSPAP data conducted by the school's instructional coordinator served to focus the selection of these school improvement strategies. Her careful study of School B's MSPAP data allowed her to recognize some recurrent student testing weaknesses, which she then translated into a set of generic instructional strategies that were tailored to the test and applicable across the curriculum. The school's intensive focus on MSPAP was affirmed by the instructional coordinator when she noted: "I could very confidently say that MSPAP is driving every single action and thought in this building" (B-20).

Teacher in-service training and weekly team meetings provided the settings for instruction in generic test-taking strategies that virtually all teachers incorporated into their daily lessons. These strategies were designed to promote student acquisition of skills needed to do well on the MSPAP test, such as writing persuasive arguments and answering reading comprehension questions in paragraph form. Using these "tricks" to crack the performance-based format of the MSPAP (B-20), teachers instructed students in how to structure responses so that they met MSPAP grading standards. One teacher explained:

> Now I am just trying to teach some strategies here for the MSPAP. I know that when they grade the MSPAP, it is an assembly-line process. And I am thinking, I am just personally thinking then if they see a good topic sentence on these sentences, that would help squeeze some points for us. (B-19)

Several teachers conveyed their sentiment that the school had become much more "test focused" (B-3, B-6, B-20) at the expense of subject content. In fact, the school's tremendous emphasis on generic test preparation strategies was made evident in the thick instructional handbook developed by the instructional coordinator. This handbook, filled with a veritable alphabet soup of tips and pointers designed to orient instruction toward building MSPAP skills, was distributed to every teacher in the building at the beginning of the 1999–2000 schoolyear. Concerning the handbook's purpose, the instructional coordinator commented: "The kind of work that is happening here is naming skills, very specific skills, that can be applied to each content. Content-specific skills? No" (B-20). Most teachers reported that they believed the strategies to be helpful in the classroom, and their use was widely observed during classroom observations. In fact, 92% of School B teachers surveyed reported using new instructional methods in their classrooms as a result of the school's reconstitution-eligible status.

While teachers reported their satisfaction with many of the new strategies brought to the school after being placed on probation, several expressed concern that the constant focus on MSPAP reduced their ability to teach the basic competency skills they believed their students needed. Concerning this issue, one sixth-grade teacher commented that the state "is trying to get higher-order thinking when the kids are having a hard enough time with the basic skills. They're making kids jump levels, and they're missing a lot in the middle . . . missing the foundation" (B-14). When asked about this issue, 70% of those teachers surveyed believed that teaching to the MSPAP required them to neglect skills that were needed by their students. Indeed, the inherent conflict in the state's requirement that students must be equally well prepared for both the MSPAP and the MFTs did not go unnoticed by teachers. As one seventh-grade teacher noted: "We have the Functionals through the state, which are all multiple-choice and basic. And then [the students] have MSPAP next year. So what do you want me to prepare for? You can't teach kids one way, and give them a different format" (B-9).

In addition to test-taking skills for the performance-based test, the school focused on reading remediation for the vast majority of its students reading below grade level with the help of a reading lab and an additional period of reading for all seventh graders. This scheduling change meant that approximately 10 minutes was shaved off the class time of other subjects. Teachers of other subjects expressed frustration with this schedule change because, despite the shorter class periods, they were still expected to cover the same curriculum. In addition, the capacity of the reading lab was insufficient. Because it accommodated only 15 students at a time, teachers of all subjects were required to teach reading to those who could not be in the lab. Some of those teachers, while supporting students' use of the lab, felt ill equipped to teach reading and concluded that the classroom portion of the reading period tended to be of little use for the students:

> What happens is I'm actually a babysitter for reading. Because half of my class goes to the reading lab for 15 or 20 minutes, so they leave, they go there, they come back. The other half goes down, and there is no way that I'm teaching reading . . . there's a true interruption in my lesson (if I had one), but I don't bother to do one because it's just not good. (B-11)

After the school was identified as low-performing, School B's administration worked hard to create what it considered a consistent learning environment for its students. This consistency was built around the establishment of uniform practices for classroom teachers governing lesson planning, pedagogy, and classroom appearance. Examples of these standardized practices included the following: that lesson plans promoting the acquisition of MSPAP skills be written daily and collected weekly for administrative review; that course objectives, warm-up, and closure activities be written daily on the chalkboard; that timers be used to time student classroom activities; and that student materials and MSPAP words/rubrics be hung on classroom walls and changed regularly.

As noted earlier, this standardization was met with mixed reviews. Some teachers believed that consistency was helpful because it allowed students to become familiar with a uniform set of expectations. As one teacher noted: "This administration is trying to get things together, they are trying to have all teachers on one accord and not be on 'I'm doing my thing, you do your thing.' . . . And we are working on that; trying to get a cohesiveness" (B-2). However, other teachers resisted these measures, with one teacher even going so far as to consider the uniformity as potentially damaging to students: "I think that seeing it done more than one way fosters creativity in a kid. I mean, if you're saying this is the way to do it, this is the way . . . then you don't have those kids with powered perspectives" (B-10). Others considered increased control of instruction as superfluous and not very substantive:

A lot of times we feel we're being watched all the time. Which is kind of insulting, especially with people who have been teaching for 20 years. . . . Now all of a sudden they have to write up these picayune little lesson plans, and they have to have certain things on the walls. Not that the kids read them or anything, but, you know, it's just another thing that we're required to do, another thing that's going to take up our time. (B-16)

Teachers worried about the fact that they were expected to have a different lesson plan each day, complete with new objectives and activities, despite their personal belief that their students might need to focus on the same work for more than one day. However, whether or not they were in agreement, they tried to exhibit the structures and activities that the principal would check. Several teachers said they felt stressed about the fact that they might be "caught with [their] pants down" during these inspections (B-11). As one teacher noted:

You never know when the principal is going to come and check the [lesson plan]. He checks to make sure it's completed. Makes sure that the correct date is on there. He's making sure that it's different basically every day. He wants papers up . . . graded papers, corrected class work, corrected homework on the board and on the walls. And he's checking for different posters we should have up to enrich the kids. I think he's checking for timers, making sure we're using the timers and making sure that we're closing the lesson. (B-6)

As a result of its probationary status, School B was the recipient of approximately $150,000 in school improvement funds. The money bought additional library books and financed after-school activities, but it was primarily used to finance additional instructional specialist positions, technology, a reading lab, and a comprehensive school reform model. Virtually all teachers were aware that the school had been the recipient of a large amount of funding, and they responded positively to the variety of new resources and assistance. However, as mentioned previously, they expressed regret that the school needed to be labeled low-performing in order to obtain them.

When the district in year 2 of probation mandated the adoption of a comprehensive reform design for all middle schools on probation, the school selected a technology-based model that was expensive and required the purchase of new hardware. Although anticipated to be the centerpiece of school improvement for the 1999–2000 schoolyear, the required computers were not purchased and installed until the end of the year. The delay was initially caused by the county's incoming school superintendent, who refused to release school funds until she had conducted a detailed review of the school system's 1999–2000 budget. The computers were further delayed when the vendor with whom the school had placed its order suddenly stopped doing business with the district because its account had fallen into arrears. Nevertheless, the administration moved forward with all scheduled in-service activities for teachers. This proved to be a controversial action among School B's faculty. While most teachers noted their interest in being able to incorporate technology into the classroom, they found it difficult to incorporate the model without Internet access. As a result, the training was viewed by many teachers as simply a waste of their time: "Without the computers in the classroom, we don't understand why we're meeting with [the model consultants]. What they expect us to do is not realistic" (B-14). Interestingly, while the model actually encompassed a variety of activities in addition to the use of classroom computers—such as project-based instruction and portfolio assessment—teachers focused almost exclusively on its technological aspects. The model managed to help a few teachers implement group projects focusing on high-interest topics such as the portrayal of teens in the media. However, it was telling that these teachers were directed to implement these creative group projects designed to promote higher-order thinking skills only after the completion of that year's MSPAP preparation and examinations.

In addition to test preparation and model-specific in-services, the school also provided staff development aimed at the upgrading of teacher skills, particularly for its large group of young and inexperienced teachers who fluctuated from year to year. Each Wednesday afternoon the master teacher offered teacher-training sessions covering such diverse topics as how to write a lesson plan, classroom management, and active learning strategies. Many of the more experienced teachers noted the decidedly "new teacher" bent to these in-services. As one experienced teacher noted: "The professional development that we have . . . I believe is working tremendously, especially with the younger teachers" (B-10). More experienced teachers, however, did not find these in-services particularly relevant to their needs. Some of these teachers expressed frustration with the lack of focus on content:

> We have several workshops here, and they're mainly on lesson planning, long-range planning, but it is for all of the content and doesn't really focus on that one subject, like social studies, for example. It doesn't focus on one particular subject matter as far as things that you can take to your class. (B-6)

Summary

In summary, probation increased administrative control at School B, but control came with a smiling face. The principal was warm and paternal but had made it clear that they—he with the rest of the school—had their backs against the wall. The demands of accountability were a given, and conversations in meetings revolved around how to implement the principal's directions. The instructional specialists were accommodating and always full of ideas, but the teachers knew that their proposals were what the principal wanted to get done. Teachers at School B felt controlled and supported. Many of our interviewees empathized with the principal's difficult position, they "understood" that accountability dictated stronger measures, and they appreciated the sense of direction that was provided for them, but at the same time many wished to escape the pettiness and pressure and work somewhere else. After the first year of probation, and despite the school's success in raising test scores, 70% of the surveyed teachers were contemplating leaving the school.

In designing its improvement strategies, School B closely followed the demands of the accountability system and fulfilled district mandates. Test preparation strategies, reading remediation, a mandated comprehensive school reform project, and the basic support of inexperienced teachers were the strategic foci. The caliber of support received from the instructional specialists backed up by the principal's regular classroom visits opened classroom doors and made teachers' instruction subject to external intervention. It is noteworthy, however, that these interventions were restricted to elements of instruction that could easily be monitored by the principal or covered by the specialists' areas of expertise. Strategies resulted in add-ons to the regular instructional programs, which remained largely untouched. The strategies, however, ran into implementation problems and trade-offs that hampered the school's forceful response. The school benefited from additional resources. Without them probation would have been met with much more teacher dissatisfaction, which remained high despite the fact that the school was moving.

SCHOOL C—A MOVING ELEMENTARY SCHOOL

School C, located in the same district as School B, was the moving elementary school in the sample. Approximately 65% of the school's overwhelmingly African American student population qualified for free or reduced-price lunches, and 100% received Title I services at the time we conducted the study. The school was highly transient, distinguished by a student mobility rate exceeding 50% and high teacher turnover. The year preceding School C's placement on the probation list, 12 veteran teachers had left the school and been replaced largely by new and inexperienced teachers. The school was also characterized by extreme overcrowding, with 13 portable classrooms used to capture student overflow.

Here, as in School B, the school's long-term principal had survived the low-performance designation. When School C was identified as reconstitution-eligible in 1998, the school's performance scores had hit the bottom for the entire county. Its severe overcrowding and fractured staff relations only served to exacerbate School C's woes. Upon identification, the district changed the school's attendance zone and hence solved the overcrowding problem. By the next schoolyear, student enrollment had declined by 25% and the student–teacher ratio had improved considerably. Nonetheless, a good number of faculty members transferred out of the school yet again.

The state's announcement of School C's low-performance status did not come as a surprise to most teachers. In fact, the teachers and administrators welcomed the status because of the money and help it would bring, but most abhorred the way it was communicated to them and to the public. "This action is as a synonym for help and was completely misnamed," commented one teacher (C-3). School C was featured in the local press as one of the worst elementary schools in the county. However, School C's placement on probation did surprise the veteran principal, who only a few months before had received a recognition from the state for the improvements made by the school during the 1995–1996 schoolyear. The principal saw teacher turnover as a main reason for the negative turn of events. Disappointed, he commented: "I gave them opportunity for staff development. I sent them places to grow. And when they get better opportunities, they leave. . . . And I lost them all. . . . I had to start all over from scratch with a bunch of new people, and it did not work" (C-1).

School C's principal became proactive once again in the face of the probation threat. One of his first activities was teacher recruitment. Using his own networks in the community, he successfully recruited teachers with high professional standards from neighboring parochial schools. He also set out to implement a series of school improvement strategies focusing on test score diagnostics and curriculum reform. Though tailored to the elementary grades, the school improvement strategies selected by School C were similar to those described for School B. For example, the principal delegated the role of instructional leader to his district-funded specialists and backed up their authority with classroom visits, write-ups, and paternalistic control. He was lucky to have found a reading specialist who was not only able to hold her own in the area of testing diagnostics but who also went on to prepare daily lesson plans for all primary grade teachers aligned with both MSPAP and the county's reading curriculum. Teachers praised the effect. A veteran teacher with 30 years in education and more than 15 years at the school said:

> Until the school was named recon-eligible, there wasn't any systematic effort to train teachers for teaching new methodology required for successful performance on the MSPAP, such as cooperative learning, problem solving, and others. Curriculums were also not aligned with the MSPAP. (C-4)

In addition to these curricular changes, several other organizational changes were made at School C. A master schedule and departmentalization of fifth-grade instruction were introduced. Common planning time for grade teachers was provided to help foster collegial interaction. Professional development for the many inexperienced teachers was high on the school's agenda, and teachers praised it as very useful.

As in School B, the combination of assistance and paternal enforcement opened classroom doors and, in the case of this school, instructional strategies penetrated even more deeply into the daily classroom routines of primary grade classrooms. Novice teachers became eager recipients of the reading specialist's help. In the upper grades, however, the influence of instructional specialists on the classroom was weaker. Some teachers expressed resentment about the new pressures and disillusionment about the new requirements that mandated closely following weekly lesson plans and prescribed curriculum, primarily because they did not afford teachers the time needed to adjust instruction to students' needs or motivate them to learn. Despite these critiques, the school was able to raise test scores substantially in 2 consecutive years. Notwithstanding the school's success, however, by the end of the 1999–2000 schoolyear, teacher morale was low. Out of 30 classroom teachers in 1997–1998, only 8 could still be found in the school at the beginning of the 2000–2001 schoolyear; of those 8, 4 were kindergarten teachers. The principal had announced his retirement and the key instructional specialist her leaving, dimming the prospects of the school's improvement trajectory.

PATTERNS OF DEVELOPMENT IN THE MOVING SCHOOLS

Patterns of organizational development due to probation were very similar in the two moving schools. Principals under pressure faced a faculty of largely skeptical senior teachers and many younger inexperienced teachers who were only mildly mobilized by probation. The principals became proactive and, despite their own doubts, accepted the accountability system and its incentives as givens. They assembled a leadership team and increased control over those features of instruction that could be easily monitored. Test preparation, reading remediation, and the implementation of district-mandated curricula and reform measures were strategic foci. Debate was curtailed, and learning and inquiry were heavily concentrated in the leadership teams. Vigorous, perhaps even rigid, top-down management moved improvement processes forward. Despite the schools' success in raising test scores, teacher dissatisfaction was high, and even key proponents of school improvement were prone to leave the school.

The paths taken by the two moving schools were due to unique site factors and external support. Internally, the principals' strength of leadership, the savvy of instructional specialists, and the higher sense of organizational cohesion, collegiality, and faculty skill relative to the stuck schools were key factors, notwithstanding the overall fragility and social instability of even the moving schools. But district conditions and policies played a role as well. Because reconstitution-eligible schools were only a small percentage of all schools in this large district, the district was able to concentrate funds and human resources on these schools. On the survey, twice as many respondents in the two moving schools (50%) compared to the two stuck schools (25%) considered new funds and new personnel as essential for the improvement of their school. This support enabled the division of labor between the principal as the overarching authority and the specialists as the instructional leaders. Furthermore, the district operated an office of school improvement that was in close touch with the schools and provided technical assistance on MSPAP-related strategies and interventions, but the office also issued clear directives, at times to the displeasure of schools. Lastly, district officials protected seasoned principals, who were given a chance to learn.

CHAPTER 5

Schools Stuck in Low Performance

WITH KIM CURTIS

IN THE SCHOOLS STUCK in low performance, teachers, in the aggregate, were less engaged and exerted less effort compared to the moving schools. At least for the period of the study, we could not discern a strategic response to probation and found the faculty overall dispirited and in disarray. This chapter describes the organizational development of three Maryland schools. Schools D and E were previously contrasted with the two moving schools. The third school, School A, is added here as an example of a school that experienced some positive movement during the study period but ultimately failed to improve. All three schools have in common that they were unable to raise their test scores on the MSPAP, the central assessment of the Maryland accountability system, during the study period.

We will trace the different developments of the schools after they were "named." School E, experiencing a remarkable trajectory, is described here at length. After an initial ray of hope and spike of improvement that preceded our study, School E was in precipitous decline and eventually collapsed almost entirely. By contrast, School D, which will be described only very briefly, had been a rock-bottom performer from the inception of the Maryland accountability system and remained so over the years, making very little movement despite probation. Finally, School A, which was not included in the earlier statistical analysis because it wavered between movement and decline, responded with vigor but moved astray into what we called "pathological rigidity."

SCHOOL E—AN ELEMENTARY SCHOOL STUCK IN DECLINE

School E had to cope with a district context that was markedly different from the district in which the two moving schools were located. School E was located

---

We wish to acknowledge Betty King's contribution to field work and analysis for Schools D and E.

in a district that saw about half of its schools identified as reconstitution-eligible over a period of 5 years. Additional funding for these schools decreased as the ranks of schools on probation swelled until the district consolidated reconstitution funds into its general assistance for schools with special needs.

School E was an elementary school located in an exceptionally poor inner-city neighborhood. Outside the school, empty lots and vacant houses invited drug activity and other crimes. The entire row of houses behind the school was virtually vacant and served as a haven for drug dealers. While the exterior surroundings of the school were clearly indicative of an impoverished and neglected neighborhood, the school itself provided a welcome contrast to this bleak landscape.

The school's students were overwhelmingly African American and poor. A Title I school at the time of the study, 90% to 100% of the student body qualified for free or reduced-price lunches; 25% were classified as special education students. In terms of mobility, the combined student entry and exit rate hovered around the 50% mark. This combination of extremely high poverty, special education, and transience made the teaching and learning environment at School E very challenging.

The high rate of teacher turnover at School E only served to compound the school's inability to provide a stable learning environment for its students. Teachers and administrators alike recounted stories of drastic measures taken to compensate for the staffing shortages caused by numerous teacher departures. For example, during the 1998–1999 schoolyear the lead technology teacher, who was already spending 2 weeks out of each month teaching third grade, was forced to give up these duties in order to take on a first-grade class after four first-grade teachers suddenly left at midyear. As she noted: "We're pulling people from everywhere trying to fill in the gaps" (E-15). The situation did not improve the subsequent schoolyear when, in what had become a familiar pattern, two third-grade teachers left the school by December. Again, the principal was forced to reassign teachers and hire long-term substitutes lacking educational backgrounds to accommodate the deficit. In general, School E hired young, inexperienced, and frequently unqualified teachers to replace departing teachers. During the 1997–1998 schoolyear, 53% of the school's teachers possessed between 1 and 5 years of teaching experience. By the following schoolyear, this number had risen to 78%. Among these teachers, average experience amounted to just 1.6 years. Even more troubling was the fact that of the 14 new teachers hired that year, only 2 met district certification standards and just 1 had a background in elementary education.

With so many new and inexperienced staff members arriving at the school each year, the administration was forced to continually introduce a new cohort of teachers to MSPAP techniques and objectives. As a result, the school was prevented from developing a stable cadre of well-trained professionals capable of providing the type of instruction needed for its students to meet the state's rigorous achievement standards. A quote from the 1999–2000 school improvement plan sums up the school's persistent instability: "A review of the mobility data indicates that the overall effect is that every year we start with new students and staff." By 2000, just 8 of the school's 32 staff members had been at School E when it was placed on probation in 1995. Even the principal, who for years had provided the school's only main source of stability, had left.

Leadership and Interactions

While at the time of the study probation or reconstitution was becoming a routine phenomenon in the district, School E had been one of the first elementary schools in the state to be "hit" with the label in 1994. As interviewees recounted, the low-performance designation was a shock. Educators at School E felt publicly exposed as failures, stigmatized by colleagues from other schools in the district, and fearful for their future in the district. At the same time, they felt unfairly singled out. Theirs was a school with a particularly challenging student population—the "special ed magnet" of the city, as one respondent quipped—and they did not consider their performance as teachers to be below par when compared with other schools.

The principal's first reaction to the label of reconstitution-eligibility was defiance. In a defensive posture, she rallied both her staff and the community against the unfair state measure. But soon she began to explore reasons for the school's low test scores. The MSPAP was a fairly new test at the time. As a former full-time staff developer for the district, she studied the test and realized that the performance-based pedagogy underlying the test was virtually unknown at her site. Soon she began training her staff in this area. In addition, she used budget funds and grant awards to staff the school with additional instructional specialists. These forms of staff development and training became the school's main improvement intervention. Teachers and administrative staff members alike praised the principal for seeing "the big picture," and bringing this vision of school improvement to School E.

Over time, the principal garnered districtwide attention for her staff development activities. Increasingly regarded as an expert by district administrators, she spent a great deal of time helping other schools on probation create their own staff development programs and school improvement plans. However, while she was busy helping other schools in the district to improve, progress at School E stalled.

She was not a controlling manager at her school. Within the administrative office, it was the secretary, not the principal, who provided the most visible and authoritative presence. Frequently away from School E attending to district training activities, the principal relied on her administrative secretary to run the building in her absence. In response, the secretary willingly took on managerial responsibility for a wide variety of activities ranging from playground supervision to class dismissal to monitoring of teacher attendance. This was resented by many faculty members, who criticized the principal's lack of interaction with the staff on a day-to-day basis and described her as uncommunicative.

Student discipline was an area of great frustration, one where administrative attention, according to many interviewees, was lacking. Students "stand up here and sass you like a dog" voiced a frustrated teacher, and another one commented that "this is a place where you're educated. My job is not to yell all day"(E-12). A scant 10% of those teachers completing a confidential survey believed that rules for student behavior were consistently enforced. Without backup from the administration, many teachers felt that punishing their students was a futile effort. Some "just stopped sending students to the office" because "they just sit there or help out in the office" (field notes). Additionally, more than one teacher wondered why the in-house detention program outlined in the school improvement plan had not been implemented.

Beyond fairly common complaints about the management of the school, the vast majority of teachers at School E also reported substantial levels of conflict among the teaching staff. The rift between teachers was particularly strong between groups of old and new staff members. Interestingly, the principal's leadership strategies may have contributed to this "intergenerational" acrimony. The principal recalled that she used the newer staff as a "catalyst" to spur on the established staff to change practices. She acknowledged that as a result of this approach, "some of the seasoned teachers would take pot shots" at the newer teachers because "they knew that these young up-starts were setting a pace and a level of expectancy that they weren't going to be able to meet" (E-7). However, instead of raising the level of staff performance across the school, this strategy appears simply to have led to the departure of some of the school's more experienced teachers. As the principal noted, these more experienced teachers "began to drop away faster than the new ones" (E-7). Teachers highlighted the "closed-door" mentality pervading the school: "My classroom; I shut my doors; these are my walls. I'll fix the 20 students here" (E-3). Across the seven Maryland schools in the sample, School E had the lowest mean ratings for collegiality and the lowest perception of faculty capacity.

Strategies for Improvement

As a response to probation, School E set out to implement a number of strategies aimed at improving MSPAP performance. These strategies can be grouped into three broad categories: staff development, district-mandated instructional programs, and technology.

As was mentioned earlier, the major thrust of School E's school reform strategies focused on staff development, which the principal designed and pioneered. For this, the principal relied on a half-day per week of release time for staff development activities provided by the district to conduct school-based training activities. District funding cuts during the 1997–1998 school-year had eliminated these early release days. The school's frustration at the district's move is evident in the following passage from the school improvement plan:

> Because of a lack of release days for school-based staff development, new staff members are not receiving in-depth benefit from training, follow-up, coaching, discussion, action research, and professional exchange. The impact has affected all facets of the programming at [School E]. (SIP 1999–2000)

In addition, the district began to require teachers to attend off-site professional development sessions conducted by district training coordinators. Convinced that school-based training was necessary for her staff's success, the principal was left with the task of reconciling her own training agenda with that of the district. The result was an extensive staff development schedule for School E's teachers. However, School E's trouble with implementing its professional development agenda cannot be seen solely as the result of changes in district policy. Its school-based training program also suffered because the principal was called out more frequently while, at the same time, teacher turnover increased and training needs compounded. School E's exceedingly high rate of annual teacher turnover meant that the school received little sustained benefit from its training initiatives.

During the 1998–1999 schoolyear, School E also implemented a new district-mandated unified reading program that focused on phonics for grades K–2 and literature for grades 3–5. Trade books were purchased for each classroom library to supplement this effort. In addition, the district mandated a 150-minute reading/language arts block. During this time period, students were supposed to engage in uninterrupted reading, with a concentration on phonetic awareness for primary grades and higher-order thinking skills for the intermediate grades.

On the whole, the administration and staff welcomed this unified, phonics-based reading initiative and believed that it responded to the needs of their students. However, some instructional specialists voiced concerns about the ability of teachers to adequately implement the new program. Indeed, even though representatives from the publishing company were available for on-site training and consultation, a number of teachers appeared to have difficulties using the new program. For example, even though the program was scripted on a day-to-day basis, some teachers had trouble keeping pace with the curriculum. Other teachers had trouble managing the script, either reading it word for word or not being able to use their cue cards correctly. Packaged programs for math and science instruction, known as MARS and STARS, were also used at School E. While these programs were designed to emphasize problem-solving and higher-order thinking skills in accordance with MSPAP requirements, teachers reported that instruction in these subjects was frequently sacrificed due to the school's emphasis on reading and language.

The administration viewed the addition of technology, featured prominently in its school improvement plan, as an integral aspect of School E's improvement process. To this end, the school purchased two computer labs and created a new position for a lead technology teacher to help oversee all technology interventions. In addition, computer terminals were available in every classroom. However, training teachers to integrate computers into their instruction proved to be difficult. Frustrated with teachers' reluctance to use the classroom computers, the technology specialist commented that it was a challenge "just to get teachers to turn [them] on" (E-3). Implementation was abruptly curtailed midyear when staffing changes eliminated the technology specialist position and the technology teacher was forced to fill a vacancy in the first grade. The pervasive instability of the school's teaching staff made any efforts beyond covering the basic curriculum a luxury the school could not afford. As a result, the principal had to do without the stable leadership team needed to fulfill the increasingly dire training needs of the faculty in basic classroom operations and in carrying out the new prescriptive programs.

Denouement

In the first years after identification, test scores rose moderately with the staff development strategy. The proportion of students scoring "satisfactory" on the MSPAP in fifth-grade math rose from zero to about 25% and in reading from roughly 2% to almost 8%, but by 1999 the reading scores were down to zero and the math scores had reverted to almost zero.

At the time the research team entered the school, awareness of, and concern for, reconstitution-eligibility was low. Many faculty members were struggling with new curricula, and school improvement activities were carried out in a perfunctory manner. The strategic focus was still on training and the digestion of the new externally mandated programs, but administrative follow-up was missing. At the end of the 1998–1999 schoolyear, the district decided to transfer the principal. Instead, she chose to take early retirement. A group of experienced teachers who had in many respects been the backbone of the school's improvement efforts also left. The school began the 1999–2000 school year with a new and inexperienced principal and many new uncertified teachers. Halfway into the schoolyear, the state decided to actually reconstitute the school and turn it over to a private school management company beginning the following schoolyear. For the remainder of the year, teacher morale sank to an all-time low as resentment and anxiety rose. MSPAP scores bottomed out.

SCHOOL D—A MIDDLE SCHOOL STUCK IN STAGNATION

School D was a distinctly inner-city middle school located near a blighted part of town. Housed in a building in dire need of basic repairs, it was one of the first middle schools to be designated as reconstitution-eligible by the state. During its 5 years of probation, School D's MSPAP scores hovered around the performance level that had brought it to the attention of the state in the first place, although slight increases in scores were posted in some years. Throughout the probationary period, principals turned over fairly rapidly, leaving little mark on the operation of the school. If School D had ever shown a more spirited response to probation, there was no trace of that during the time of our field work. For teachers the supposed urgency of probation was simply submerged among the many other concerns for daily order and survival. This teacher's attempt to explain what probation meant to her is rather typical for School D:

> I don't know whether I think it's a threat. . . . Let me say it like this: What it imposes is something that you can't see, and it's kind of like (and I call it a pressure), it's kind of like a pressure that you know is there. The pace is accelerated. The amount of paperwork is quadrupled . . . and the kind of anticipation is kind of heightened. But . . . all of that is stuff you can't really see except for the paperwork. And it's, it kind of makes it feel like you know something's going on, but you can't quite put your finger on it. (D-3)

When we first entered School D, we encountered a dispirited principal who felt he had barely made a dent in his school during his one-year tenure. Frustrated by flat test scores, district inaction on the most basic building repairs, and feuding with the faculty over discipline and parental participation in decision making, he was counting the days until he was replaced. He knew that he had failed to bring the faculty together and raise test scores, and he knew the consequences. The next principal showed very little urgency or concern for change. He said that he would study the school the first year and then take his steps. He was liked, but he was also known to take his breaks with other teachers, smoking under a tree off school grounds. He left much of the day-to-day administration to his grade-level assistant principals. As a result, the school established very few consistent policies across grade levels.

The school's central challenge was student discipline. A schoolwide discipline system, demanded by vocal parts of the faculty, was never established. All attempts at instituting discipline policies failed over the 2 years we studied School D. The result was a school under siege where yelling and visible signs of exasperation were common and where teachers solved discipline problems by sending students into the halls and students roamed the halls unsupervised. Rather than improving discipline, the opposite happened when the new principal lost funding for hall monitors and an in-house suspension center. His tenure ended with an acrimonious faculty meeting during which faculty members aired their raw frustrations with his inaction.

School D wrestled with basic issues of organizational disorder and mismanagement, lack of faculty continuity and cohesion, and lack of student discipline. The school was divided and rudderless. The tenure of two principals ended with serious conflicts among faculty and between faculty and administration. Teacher turnover remained very high from year to year. After 5 years of very little change, probation was becoming a meaningless label. Many teachers were dissatisfied, increasingly inexperienced, and uncommitted to the school. Schoolwide issues, such as probation, were sources of conflict and had become frustrating distractions for classroom teachers, many of whom reacted by withdrawal:

> The bottom line is I know I have a group of kids for me to [make them] learn. I will focus on teaching them. That's my perspective. As far as the administration, that's their responsibility for reconstitution. (D-20)

Even though disorder and fragmentation prevailed, teachers succeeded in increasing the school's scores on the state's basic skills tests, on which School D had had exceptionally low scores.

SCHOOL A—PATHOLOGICAL RIGIDITY

First caught off-guard by probation, then taking vigorous steps to improve, School A saw its prospects dim toward the end of the study when vigor turned into pathological rigidity.

School A was located in the same district as the two moving schools. In some ways it was very much like School B, the moving middle school, but it was larger by about 250 students, drew from slightly poorer communities, and did not have a magnet program. School A toiled under the same probation regime and received the same external support from the district as its more successful neighbor, School B, but it did not manage to take off even though it employed many of the same strategies as did School B.

Leadership and Interactions

At the time the reconstitution verdict reached School A in the spring of 1998, the school was led by an inexperienced team of administrators who were new to the task of running a school and had just been assigned to the school in September of the previous year. They were hard-pressed to deal with School A's severe problems with student discipline. Up until the spring of the 1997–1998 schoolyear, the faculty had written a total of 791 discipline referrals, statistically almost one referral per student. The school had imposed 180 suspensions affecting about 14% of the student population, with the last, suspension-prone quarter of the schoolyear still outstanding. In 1996–1997, roughly a quarter of the students had been suspended without much effect. Veteran teachers reported that discipline had been a problem in the school for a long time.

In February of 1998, the state announced that the school would become reconstitution-eligible. With that new status came a whole slew of new requirements, most notably the writing of the school improvement plan to which the principal dedicated herself while still trying to get her bearings in the school. The school managed to write a plan that won praise from local administrators, but internally it was introduced to the faculty as a fait accompli. Interestingly, student discipline was not a major focus of the plan. While the principal was busy fulfilling the new probation requirements, school order slowly disintegrated. By the end of the year, despite the principal's publicly voiced conviction that the school would turn around, teacher morale was low, expectations for improvements had evaporated, and dissension had reached the administrative team. Contemplating leaving, one of the vice principals voiced her helplessness and disapproval of the principal's lack of skill as a disciplinarian. The schoolyear ended with a mass exodus of about half the staff, most of them seasoned teachers and among them a large number of science teachers credentialed in their field, some highly involved teachers, and at least one plan writer. Reconstitution was mentioned as one of the reasons for exit, but it paled in the face of daily problems of student discipline. One teacher who chose to stay commented about her leaving colleagues, "Nobody wants to be associated with a sinking ship" (field notes). Test scores declined even further during this first year of probation.

In the following schoolyear, the district installed a new principal who had previously achieved performance improvements in a similar school that had not yet reached the stage of probation. She was allowed to assemble her own administrative team: two assistant principals, a master teacher, and a coordinator for school improvement activities whose position was funded out of the school's probation budget.

Although it was not a focus of the state-approved school improvement plan, discipline became the immediate focus of the new principal, who lost no time tackling the problem. At a faculty meeting early in the year, she introduced her plan, which involved a strict hall pass, escort, and lunch supervision system. When one of the teachers who had been at the school the previous year wanted to voice a concern about the plan, the teacher was interrupted and told in no uncertain terms by the principal "to follow the policy." All discussion ceased thereafter. The new discipline policies were thus set in motion, carried out by a compliant, though in parts grumbling, faculty and enforced by a determined administration. In time, student discipline improved. The principal and her new administrative team succeeded in imposing a sense of orderly conduct upon the school that had previously been absent—no small feat.

Yet these drastic measures exacted a heavy price from the organization in terms of time and human resources. A description of lunchtime may illustrate what it took for the school to maintain order and discipline. Because of its modular schedule, lunchtime at School A was an affair that lasted for 2½ hours, during which time the various teams brought their classes to the cafeteria. We observed a typical lunchtime walk of an eighth-grade class. Ten minutes before the end of the lesson, the teacher lined up her class in preparation for their walk to the cafeteria. Slowly the students filed out of the room, forming a single line under the watchful eye of the teacher. The class began walking slowly toward the cafeteria, hugging the wall and stopping at every corner and every clock, being constantly reminded by their teacher to behave and to stay in line. The class journeyed along one long hallway, a staircase, and another long hallway. As it got closer to the cafeteria, it encountered another group of students coming from the opposite direction and passing by in single file alongside the opposite wall, being constantly monitored by their teacher. Upon arrival at the cafeteria, the students seated themselves at their regular benches. They ate in the same seating arrangement every day. Walking around and contact with other groups of students was not permitted.

The cafeteria also served as an auditorium. During lunchtime, one of the vice principals occupied the stage with a microphone. As the students sat down at their tables, the escort duty of the teacher ceased and the students came under the watchful eyes of the vice principal and seven other adults, among them guidance counselors and security guards. "Young man, sit down, sit down!" the vice principal exclaimed through the microphone. This alerted one of the adults on the floor to approach the culprit. The student quickly sat down. One of the students in the group wanted to use the restroom. She was required to ask one of the security guards and was then escorted by one of them to the location and back to her seat.

After about 20 to 30 minutes, lunchtime was over for the observed group of students. Ms. L, the vice principal, blew a whistle. "This is the signal for you to be quiet. . . . You need to be quiet for dismissal," she exclaimed with emphasis into her microphone. The huge cafeteria immediately quieted down. As Ms. L dismissed students by rows, the teachers were on hand again to escort them back to their classes in the same familiar fashion. Students again lined up at the wall and, stopping at every corner and clock, slowly moved back to their instructional area.

At School A, teachers took their substantial hall and escort duties seriously. Administrators were constantly patrolling the halls, walkie-talkies in hand, monitoring students and teachers. Security guards, guidance counselors, and administrators were constantly on guard. During instructional periods, it was up to this group (or anybody else who could assist) to be available when a classroom teacher requested an escort for a student. Thus, to maintain a safe and orderly environment, this school found it necessary not only to expend a great amount of adult time and energy on monitoring students but also to severely restrict students' movement and unencumbered socializing. Supervision at School A was constructed as a seamless web. While the faculty seemed to have accepted the supervisory burden, if begrudgingly, a number of primarily younger faculty voiced concern in conversations that the school's restrictiveness was not age-appropriate, did not prepare students for high school, and did very little to make students internalize responsible conduct. But in the words of a staunch supporter of strict enforcement of student discipline, this argument was not valid: "In a school like this, either the adults or the students run the school" (field notes).

The main problem with the tight escort policy, however, was that it required (wo)man power that the administration often did not have at its disposal. As a result, when teachers summoned an escort for emergency situations, an escort often did not show up, leaving the teacher the option of either breaking the school rules or risking a conflict with students or parents. The administration held the line on the no-pass policy and would write up teachers who were found to have broken it, which generated much resentment among faculty. In time, this emphasis on vigorous enforcement and suppression of dissent extended to all other improvement activities. In staff meetings, teachers were "walked through" the principal's strategies. At first, this forceful management style encouraged a number of teachers to become active, and teachers conceded that order had improved, but with each new principal reprimand, teachers' dissatisfaction mounted.

By November of that year, there were clouds on the horizon. Teachers began to complain about too little input into decision making and the heavy hand of an openly disrespectful administration. A number of teachers, some of them highly involved in the school improvement process, confided that they wished to exit immediately, if they only could. The principal's "tight ship," justified with the requirements of the new accountability system, alienated a group of vocal and highly involved classroom teachers, like a teacher who wanted "to see a little piece of [herself] in this school. The principal says this is the goal, and there is only *one* way to get there" (A-13). Another teacher commented: "I think the relationship between the teachers and administration is very strained. Thus, the teachers' hands are tied behind their backs, almost . . . as if *we* are on a lock-down-type basis. I mean you can *see* it with the hallway movement"(A-8). Many of these alienated teachers transferred at the end of the schoolyear.

Strategies for Improvement

One of the first instruction-related measures of the new administration was to mandate that all teachers prepare a written lesson plan for each lesson, that test vocabulary be prominently posted in classrooms, and that the official district curriculum guide be opened to the appropriate page during each lesson (presumably indicating that teachers consulted the curriculum and that the lesson taught complied with it). Invoking the force of external authority, the principal admonished teachers to heed these clear and enforceable behaviors, which would be "monitored by the state" and would also play a role in teachers' evaluations. The writing of daily lesson plans was enforced by spot checks and, in the case of noncompliance, by written admonitions. Teachers' reactions to these new requirements were similar to those of their colleagues in School B. They complied, but experienced teachers did not see much sense in them.

An ambitious calendar of professional development was carried out. Of the 30 or so distinct in-service activities, about half were dedicated to test-related skills and preparation, such as familiarizing staff with the format of performance-based test items, teaching them how to score with rubrics, and actual scoring of practice tests (so called benchmarks). Another set of workshops addressed classroom management and the middle school child, specifically addressing the needs of the many young and novice teachers at School A.

School A had instructional specialists, but they were wrapped up in organizational tasks and school order. So they never focused strongly on instruction, and their work did not attain the sophistication of School B's instructional handbook or School C's prepared reading curriculum. A major thrust was the organization of test-simulation activities. The MSPAP required students to work in randomly assigned groups to work out performance-based problems. At School A, these random groups often dissolved into conflict during the test. It was decided that the school as a whole should practice MSPAP activities, working in random groups several times during the year.

In the 1998–1999 schoolyear, the school managed to do five simulations, three so-called benchmarks and two so-called milestones. The tasks or prompts for these practice tests were mostly provided by subject-matter district offices. The prompts were then scored by faculty members who had participated in the holistic scoring training. The scoring turned out to be very time-consuming and was paid for with additional funds. When the funds ran out, scoring ceased, with the result that the last-quarter benchmark test remained unscored. These extensive test-preparation activities were considered a necessary prerequisite for the smooth launching of the tests for both teachers and students, but they also put a tremendous burden on faculty and administration. Because of the use of the randomized group format, the regular instructional program was interrupted during times when major test-preparation activities were scheduled. The scoring of practice tests took place outside regular instructional routines. It required a great deal of time from the scoring team and from teachers on release time. Funneling back of practice test results into regular classrooms was cumbersome, since test groups and regular classrooms were not identical and only a small group of teachers was involved in the scoring. Therefore, many classroom teachers were not familiar with the meaning of the scores and their use for further instructional purposes. It is unlikely that these test-preparation schemes could have been carried out without extra funds, the willingness of staff to work overtime, and the availability of a number of hardworking teachers on release time who dedicated themselves to the task.

In the eyes of many faculty members, the frequent practicing of the test paid off. Faculty members reported that when it came time for the test, students seemed familiar with the test format and were more positively disposed toward the test than in previous years, even though, according to some teachers, many of their students were hard-pressed to complete test assignments. Test organization was smooth and orderly, and teachers knew what to expect. As a result, faculty members were expecting an increase in the school's performance scores; indeed, the school improved its scores modestly during that year. But MSPAP practice activities remained separate from regular classroom routines.

In interviews, teachers reported instances of common planning of curriculum and an exchange of materials and ideas, but a systematic approach to curriculum reform was not visible. Instructional reform amounted to mandated activities (such as lesson plans or practice tests) easily monitored by the administration. The influence of instructional specialists on classrooms remained weak.

For the 1999–2000 schoolyear, the school was forced to adopt an external comprehensive school project that was supposed to deepen instructional changes. Choosing such a project was not necessarily desired by the school. Classroom teachers lamented that the project would be "one more thing to do" on the list of additional duties, and members of the leadership team fretted that staff development monies would dry up for other purposes. The project consultants trained some teachers, and this generated a couple of ambitious student-centered projects, but in its first year at the school the project fell far short of its claim to comprehensively change the school or the classroom, according to both its detractors and supporters. The project was not helped by an atmosphere in which instructional reform came to be overshadowed by interpersonal strife between administration and faculty.

Denouement

From the point of view of many teachers, the 1999–2000 schoolyear began with a clear symbol of the administration's disregard for teachers. The faculty lounge had been converted to an administrative office so that the whole administrative team could be close to the principal, while the teachers' lounge was relocated to a small, dark space that could accommodate a soda machine and mailboxes, but very little else. Some more outspoken members of the faculty decided to form a faculty advisory council. Rather than open lines of communication, confrontation ensued. Faculty meetings were no longer held. Teachers complained about the "heavy hand" of the administration. Faculty spokespersons demanded that the principal stop rebuking teachers in public, in front of students, and over the public announcement system. They also voiced concern over the large number of "pink slips" (i.e., written admonitions that remain in the teachers' personnel files for the duration of their tenure in the district) that some members of the faculty had received for minor infractions. The outcome of this conflict was uncertain at the time data collection concluded. But it resulted in the determination by some senior faculty to finally turn their backs on the school. At the end of this schoolyear—year 3 of probation and year 2 of the current leadership—the leadership team itself was in the process of dissolving. In the open strife between faculty and administration, some of the members of the leadership team were accused of being disloyal and were counseled by the principal to seek a transfer. Test scores declined.

As at the two moving schools, Schools B and C, the principal at School A responded to probation with increased control, expectation of compliance, suppression of dissent, monitoring of surface behavior in classrooms, test preparation schemes, and professional development (primarily for the many inexperienced teachers). But unlike the situation in the two moving schools, School A started its probationary period with severe student discipline problems and an inexperienced administration. The heavy-handed leadership style of the principal and the focus of instructional specialists on organizational rather than instructional matters inhibited the school's success. A groundswell of dissatisfaction and a widespread desire to leave pervaded the school.

Over the 3 years of probation, School A never stabilized. After the first-year probation exodus, the number of nontenured teachers had risen to about 30 out of a faculty of 59. Throughout the course of the 1998–1999 and 1999–2000 schoolyears, the school was unable to fill all its positions with regular teachers. Several members of the staff either quit midyear or went on leave, among them the testing coordinator. Overall, 10 positions were in flux during the 1998–1999 schoolyear and had to be staffed by long-term or day-to-day substitutes. In the 1999–2000 schoolyear, that number rose to 13 classrooms without a stable teacher, among them four mathematics positions, which presumably had a direct negative impact on the school's test scores. Many of these classes were staffed by a stream of teachers who lasted only a short while in their assignments. All in all, only 19 certificated personnel remained at the school by the end of the 1999–2000 schoolyear out of the 65 who had been present when the school was put on probation in 1998. A number of those 19 teachers indicated their desire to leave the school at the end of the schoolyear.

PATTERNS OF DEVELOPMENT IN THE STUCK SCHOOLS

Schools got stuck for different reasons, and some were not always stuck in all parts of their operations. School E's staff development strategy worked for a while, but management of the school lacked follow-through; diminishing probation funds, time constraints on staff development, constant teacher turnover, reassignment of instructional specialists to classroom duties, and mounting training needs overwhelmed the school and depleted teachers' and administrators' energy.

In School D, none of the principals left much of a mark. In the eyes of teachers, probation was an affair relegated to the administration. More pressing problems took precedence for classroom teachers: keeping control of student behavior, compelling students to show up and learn, stemming the constant teacher turnover, and providing a supply of teachers who could make it in the school's environment. The fact that School D was not able to make visible progress in these basic areas of school operation paled by comparison to the school's concerns for probation.

Thus, as was the case in the moving schools, probation by itself was only a weak motivating force on ordinary classroom teachers in the stuck schools. Unless the principal presented probation as an urgent matter of concern, the signal was apt to be submerged in the day-to-day challenges of school life. In two of the stuck schools (D and E), principal turnover or low-impact principals doomed a school's probationary period. But pathological rigidity at the opposite end of the spectrum dissipated improvement impulses as well and led to fragmentation, as seen in School A. School A is an example of a school where the very control strategies used by the principals in the two moving schools failed because the principal carried the pressures of probation too far and in the process triggered continuous dissatisfaction among and exit by the faculty.

Principals could not do the job by themselves. Given the weak impression probation left on ordinary classroom teachers, principals needed the help of instructional specialists who could fan out into classrooms and execute the leader's plan. But in the stuck schools, these instructional specialists (e.g., school improvement resource teachers, reading specialists, testing coordinators, mentor or master teachers) were either not as effective or they were relegated to administrative or regular classroom duties.

In the end, the difference between moving and stuck schools was found less in what sorts of improvement strategies and what basic patterns of organizational interaction were chosen and more in how these interactions and strategies played out based on the managerial, instructional, and human relations skills of the people involved and the support they received from their district.

CHAPTER 6

Other Schools

IN THIS CHAPTER WE REACH BEYOND the focal cases from Maryland. Findings from the content analysis of school improvement plans help us identify more generalizable patterns that may or may not be congruent with the patterns found in the focal schools. We use data from 46 Maryland schools that represent about half of all labeled low-performing schools in Maryland as of 1998. In the second section, we explore whether the patterns of organizational development identified for the Maryland schools hold up in a different state context. We summarize the findings from Kentucky's 32 school improvement plans and four focal case study schools. The chapter ends with concluding remarks about patterns of organizational development under probation.

SCHOOL IMPROVEMENT PLANNING

School improvement plans are a widespread feature in high-stakes accountability systems. They are a mandatory feature for schools put on probation in most systems. In the two states, the departments of education treated school improvement plans (SIPs) as central to a school's path back to healthy performance. SIPs are extensive documents subject to official review and approval. Whether they were hastily thrown together or carefully crafted, these school improvement plans are vivid testimony to schools' (and districts') espoused views (Schein, 1991) about the task of school improvement. Naturally, espoused views are not necessarily implemented programs.

Ideally, the development and implementation of SIPs facilitate an effective, internalized, and self-sustained process of school improvement. We saw in the previous two chapters that schools tended to respond to probation pressures with increased administrative control and standardization. In some schools, patterns of organizational rigidity were apparent. Others were un-

---

Margaret Fee Quintero contributed to the section on organizational development in the Kentucky schools.

able to get organized and remained stuck in ineffective patterns or fragmented even further under probation. Here we describe how these patterns are reflected in the content of the 46 plans. We distinguish between patterns of managerial control and internalization. Subsequently we briefly return to our seven cases to see what processes generated such plans and how the plans were used for school improvement.

It is the putative strength of accountability systems to move ineffective schools to a higher level of effectiveness by obliging schools to work according to external standards and mandates of effective management. But organizational learning takes place when these obligations are internalized. Once internalized, they make sense to practitioners and foster goal formation, critical reflection, self-evaluation, focus, and fresh commitment.

The presumed press of accountability systems toward rationalizing school operations may result in a pattern of managerial control. In this pattern, schools characteristically align their goals to the standards of the accountability system. Goals are clear and focused on student achievement. The improvement plan uses the system's quantitative diagnostics (e.g., performance tests, required school surveys). Activities center on curriculum and instruction, and professional development is viewed as training in new skills primarily in those areas. Responsibilities for tasks are clearly assigned, but administrators and specialists on top of the organizational hierarchy carry a large burden. In the spirit of accountability, demands for new resources as well as attention to teachers' work satisfaction and motivation are deemphasized. School improvement plans are relevant as public statements of the organization and as management tools for administration and specialist teachers to leverage teacher compliance with administrators' strategies.

School improvement as an internalized process under conditions of external accountability may be associated with a number of characteristics in school improvement plans. School goals reflect the standards of the accountability system, but these will be interpreted in light of actual student achievement. The plan addresses how the school will get from the present situation of probation to lofty external standards. Needs analysis combines diagnostics based on externally generated data with internal school knowledge. Analysis of causes for shortcomings focuses on those aspects of the situation that can be internally attributed and, therefore, influenced by educators at the school. Alternatively, the school distinguishes between externally and internally caused performance barriers and marks its own responsibilities clearly. Professional development includes sharing expectations for student work and formulating commitments to internal accountability. The work of classroom teachers is directly evaluated, and work commitment is a central concern. Classroom teachers as much as the administration take responsibility for activities.

In a nutshell, content analysis and case study data suggest that school improvement planning introduces a measure of programmatic focus and alignment into schools' strategies. But the plans have only limited utility for internal school development. Rather, they signal schools' conformity with external demands. Internally, and only in the successful cases, they serve as administrative levers to forge compliance among faculty (for more details, see Mintrop & MacLellan, 2002; Mintrop, MacLellan, & Quintero, 2001).

Content Analysis

In Maryland, as in other jurisdictions, schools wrote the school improvement plans according to a template developed and required by the state. According to the Maryland SIP template, schools were to cover analysis of needs and causes of underperformance, the school's philosophy and goals, and an action plan listing strategies for improvement and individuals or groups at school responsible for implementation. We follow these broad categories in our analysis.

Analysis of Needs. Student achievement, attendance, and climate measures (student discipline) were almost exclusively mentioned as needs in schools' analyses. By comparison, needs that were not directly measured by the accountability system were also featured less. For example, lack of parental involvement was mentioned by only 11% of the schools. Data used for the diagnosis of needs were mostly quantitative (70% of all entries for *use of data*) and derived from the performance indicators required by the state. By contrast, qualitative data from interviews, self-study, or observations that might document the schools' own internal knowledge appeared very infrequently in the plans.

Causes of Decline. About 70% of all causes of decline mentioned in the 46 plans can be attributed to external factors. Typical external attributions for problems included scarce resources, high student mobility, and low-socioeconomic environment. Thirty percent of the causes mentioned were attributed internally and thus were subject to schools' efforts. Schools highlighted as internal causes shortcomings of specific teacher groups, organizational structures, limitations in teachers' skills and knowledge, and leadership weaknesses. Thus, when the schools had the opportunity to explain their shortcomings, they overwhelmingly pointed to factors over which they exerted little or no control.

Goals. In most SIPs, the goals flowed from the quantitative performance indicators set by the accountability system. These goals accounted for 91% of all entries in this section. Numeric goals were calculated in line with externally set growth targets by using a set formula. Almost all schools pledged large increases in passing rates on the state's central assessment, MSPAP, sometimes exceeding 15 percentage points a year, when in actuality Maryland schools on probation statewide increased these percentages by 3 to 5 points on average over 2 years according to our calculations. Thus, in most cases, goal formation was formulaic and schools hardly ever addressed the gulf between projected high growth and past performance records. We concluded therefore that in most schools goal formation happened in "conformity to system expectations" with "achievability doubtful."

Action Plans. The analyzed plans attested to an extensive array of activities. A set of close to 50 activities on the average amounts to a substantial reform load for a school. Activities touched on all areas of a school's operation. Curriculum and instruction activities represented slightly fewer than half of all activities. Professional development was conceived in terms of discrete classes and workshops (87%) in which teachers were trained for specific skills, rather than in terms of ongoing growth activities more organically interwoven with daily instruction.

Curriculum and instruction as well as professional development activities centered on the new challenges of the performance-based test (e.g., test language, importance of writing, portfolios, student-centered instructional strategies), on district-adopted curricula, and on new packaged instructional programs. It is to the credit of the Maryland assessment program that many of the curriculum and instruction activities aimed at upgrading the complexity of learning, rather than focusing on drill and practice alone. Teacher performance activities revolved around increased control (e.g., mandating lesson plans, tighter supervision). Strategies in the areas of governance (e.g., shared decision making), work satisfaction, and teacher commitment, however, received short shrift.

Responsibilities for implementation rested to a large degree on administrators and personnel in charge of special services (e.g., counseling office, reading specialist, resource teacher). Principals and administrative personnel were responsible for about one-third of the total number of 2,113 activities that were listed by all 46 schools. Another third fell into the responsibility of special services, while classroom teachers were only directly responsible for about one-quarter of the activities.

Evaluation. Of the 2,113 total number of activities, 45% were coded as "new" and 55% as "ongoing" (usually indicated by phrases such as "will begin" or "will continue," respectively, although the time frame was often difficult to pinpoint clearly). The 1,162 entries for ongoing activities contrasted with only 83 activity entries in the database for "progress made," a category raters were to record whenever they found incidence of a past activity or program clearly identified as having been beneficial or effective for the school. Given that a high percentage of activities carried over from one year to the next, one could have expected a more analytic or evaluative stance.

School Size. We grouped the 46 reconstitution-eligible schools in our sample according to size. We hypothesized that if SIPs were truly the product of a school's internal capacity to implement the activities listed in the plan, then one might expect small schools to list fewer activities than large schools, since small schools have fewer adults to carry out activities. The 10 largest schools in our sample had between 760 and 1,130 students; the 10 smallest ones had between 240 and 350 students. But the number of activities listed by both groups was 45 on the average, almost identical to the mean for the whole sample. Hence, size (i.e., number of personnel) was not a decisive factor in the load of activities that schools pledged to carry out in the course of one schoolyear.

Test Score Development. We further hypothesized that schools posting the largest test score gains on the MSPAP might emphasize different activities than schools with the largest declines. The 10 most improved schools in our sample posted a gain of 0.06 to 17.5 points in their composite performance index (CI) from 1997 to 1998. The 10 most declined schools posted a loss of –0.7 to –8.8 points for the same period. Yet the types of activities chosen by both groups were very similar and resembled the overall pattern of all 46 schools. This finding puts the utility of school improvement plans in doubt. When neither the number of activities planned nor the specific kinds of activities listed appear decisive for schools' performance development, the quality of implementation, rather than the quality of the written plan, seems key.

Case Study Data

We explored this situation further with the help of interview data from the seven case study schools. For most interviewees, school improvement planning was primarily seen as a requirement that one must comply with:

> It was required. I mean, that's my role, to do whatever's required. (B-12)

> I think it's more or less we didn't have a choice. I think the [SIP is] more from the administration, not necessarily the school. (G-14)

Though the plans were seen as an external requirement, some saw benefits in compiling them, particularly administrators and teachers with special assignments, like this urban elementary school principal:

What that document forced us to do was to begin to take a look at our school, and to look at it in critical areas. (E-7)

While the idea of common goals and strategies found support among some, the concomitant standardization of routines and practices was more troublesome, if not outright ludicrous, to some respondents, particularly in those schools where the principals had become more controlling, such as School B:

> For you to tell me that you want my notebook on the right-hand side of my desk, I'm not going to do it. I'm not going to, because that's just . . . and I'm not being disobedient, I'm not leaving my authority, because I have a high level of respect for authority. I respect the position. I don't always respect the person, but I always respect the position, and I'll always do it. But, I'm sorry, you do not tell me, no state person, you're not going to tell me how to organize my desk. (B-9)

In all schools the plans were written by small groups of teachers. The principals were strongly involved, but the actual writing was in most cases delegated to resource teachers who worked outside the classroom and were given release time for this task. Plan writers did not mention a substantial role of the faculty at large in the writing process. If the faculty was involved, it was less likely that they were decision makers and more likely that they were information providers. A principal in one of the middle schools described the process in this way:

> We always sent down information to let the staff know what we are working on, what's involved in it, what we need from them, what they have to submit by which date, and we get what we need in on time and then we're able to file it and go from there. (A-1)

Plan writers' and administrators' gaze was directed outward rather than inward. Passing muster with district and state authorities was their primary concern. In the interviews, planners described vividly how they repeatedly revised their drafts to accommodate various demands and suggestions from the district office. District offices, for their part, felt scrutinized by the state monitoring office and felt beholden to the state officials' standards and formats for a good plan that could finally be approved by the state board of education. Mixed messages from external reviewers made the task more burdensome. In the view of many respondents, writing the plan was a "cat and mouse game" (E-7, principal).

Writers and administrators from almost all schools reported that when the final drafts were eventually returned to the schools, the plans had been rewritten again without input from the school and content had changed substantially:

> Certain things were changed in the plan that were not originally written, which I'm assuming that the county felt should be changed, before it was admitted to the state. . . . But even prior to that, there, to me, was not enough collaboration to make that plan truly what it should have been made. (A-16)

Presumably, the review process was used to oblige schools to adopt particular views and strategies deemed correct or effective by district or state officials, a presumption that was confirmed in an interview with an official from one of the districts.

At the time of data collection, in none of the schools, with perhaps one exception, were the plans an outcome of a broad-based internal communication process that could have clarified directions and motivated actions faculty-wide. Both the tight time lines for the submission of the plans and the attitude of administrators and planners toward complying with new external mandates preempted such a process. Once the plan was written, dissemination was an administrative process or left to chance: "Well, I'm on the school improvement team, which, of course, everyone's invited to be a part of it. So, unless someone just is not wanting to be involved, they've had opportunities, and the documents have been there for them to read, in the office" (A-3).

The strong external steering of the writing process, the overwhelming concern of plan writers and administrators for passing the external review, and the abbreviated internal communication process among faculty resulted in a feeble sense of ownership of the plans at the school site. A former member of the school improvement team expressed her frustration with lack of ownership:

> I used to be on the team but I got off. . . . When [the plan] comes back, it's not your product, so that's the reason I got off because it still didn't help. It wasn't ours. We don't have a say so. That's a waste of time. All that, the school improvement plan, is just for formality. Just to say that the school has a voice in what goes on in their school, and it's not necessarily so if you're going to change it. Well, all of us have a copy of the school improvement plan. Every person that works here. But, I mean, it's rarely used, it's rarely used. In the midst of everything else we have to do, people aren't going to sit down and read through a school improvement plan. (D-24)

Sense of ownership was further diminished due to high teacher and administrator turnover. Compiling the SIP ensued when the school was identified as reconstitution-eligible in the spring; identification was based on the performance scores of the previous year. The schoolyear was almost over by the time the plan was approved. As a result, we encountered administrators and teachers who did not feel they owned the problem, since they had arrived at the school a year after the decline, and those who did not own the solution, since they had freshly arrived in the new schoolyear. Now they were "stuck" with a formally codified and officially sanctioned plan whose wisdom seemed questionable at times.

Summary

We learned from the interviews that the compilation of the plans in the seven schools was done mainly by a small core of administrators and activists. The writing process itself was fundamentally steered from outside the school. Schools were given a template that prestructured planning tasks and content. The writing was micromanaged by district and state agencies, and the final product was fine-tuned so that it reflected official preferences or could meet state board approval. While site administrators and plan writers at times felt driven by murky external expectations, faculty participation in planning was limited to the provision of information. Thus, improvement planning was embedded in a stringent accountability system whose posture was reinforced by the schools' probationary status.

A broadly based consultation process was lacking. Site administrators and teachers with special assignments, who were responsible for the lion's share of intended activities, were inclined to see the beneficial internal effects of SIPs as occasions for reflection, even though some bemoaned the extraordinary burden of writing and revising the plan. Regular classroom teachers, by contrast, exhibited very superficial knowledge of their school's SIP. A general lack of ownership of the plans, which in some schools extended to traditional leadership roles (e.g., department heads), pervaded the interviews as a theme. This dearth of knowledge and ownership notwithstanding, teachers expressed a strong willingness to comply with the plan. Some teachers explicitly stated their compliance with the admittedly unknown. Teachers accepted the SIP as a tool used by the site administration to focus the faculty and to standardize operations.

The content analysis revealed what kinds of plans were produced under these conditions. The plans showed strong signs of alignment. Site goals mimicked official quantitative performance goals, needs analysis took its cues from performance indicators, and a good portion of intended activities revolved around the state assessments and training in more pedagogically complex instruction and new mandated programs. But on the other hand, the plans were comprehensive to a fault and only loosely tailored to internal faculty capacity, perhaps creating a condition of change overload rather than strategic focus—that is, if all intended activities were implemented faithfully. Such sweeping implementation was less likely considering that the plans lacked signs of internalization. The enumeration of mainly externally attributed causes of decline read more like a plea to the public for leniency than an examination of the schools' problems—a "rational" approach, perhaps, taken by schools, which in many cases were truly embattled because of their social environment and district neglect.

ORGANIZATIONAL DEVELOPMENT IN THE KENTUCKY SCHOOLS

The four Kentucky schools that participated in the study represent a checkered past of performance in the state accountability system. Across the three biennia of the accountability system's existence, one elementary school and one middle school were reward schools during the first two biennia—that is, they met or exceeded their growth targets—but in the third biennium they fell into decline. The other two schools had been in decline for at least two biennia. Thus, akin to the Maryland selection of schools, we collected data in both newly identified and longer-term probation schools. Like the Maryland schools, the Kentucky schools were highly impacted by poverty. Students from ethnic minority backgrounds, mainly African American children, were overrepresented compared to the state as a whole.

Less Urgency

On the level of individual motivation, basic patterns were similar in schools from both states, though certain beliefs and attitudes were weighted somewhat differently. Kentucky teachers tended to be more anxious about probation (though mean differences were not statistically significant), and the pressure of probation was the number-one reason for teachers wanting to leave their school. In all likelihood, this heightened apprehension was due to fewer exit options, given labor-market conditions in areas around the Kentucky schools. Similar to their Maryland counterparts, Kentucky teachers dismissed the possibility of severe sanctions in the interviews.

Ratings for meaningfulness of accountability were low among educators from both states, but in the Kentucky schools respondents were even more critical and pessimistic. Judging from the interviews, this was most likely related to public debate about the reliability and practicality of accountability that was beginning to grip the state at the height of the study. Toward the end of the study, the state actually abandoned the initial test (Cibulka & Lindle, 2001).

School-specific factors in two of the four schools compounded teachers' deep sense of being treated unfairly by the accountability system. Both middle schools suffered from the consequences of districtwide magnet school programs that left them with the designation of a neighborhood school and resulted in a negative creaming effect for these schools. For example, School 20 experienced a large influx of special education students, above the district average, and faced a sharp increase in numbers of students living in poverty. Percentages of students eligible for free or reduced-price lunches rose from one-fourth to three-fourths over a decade, without adjustment for the school's accountability targets. One school considered itself the "district dumping ground," another the district "special ed magnet."

Kentucky teachers reported placing less importance on their success on the state assessment than did the Maryland respondents. In each of the four schools, teachers named multiple other indicators of success as being more important than performing well on the state assessments, including student success in class, parental or administrative praise, affection from students, and even scores on the Comprehensive Test of Basic Skills (CTBS), a test that was not even a component of the accountability formula. In both middle schools, the highly skilled educators (HSEs) commented that one of the greatest impediments to reform was that the teachers did not feel the test was fair and thus found other measures to serve as indicators of their own success.

In the four Kentucky schools, teachers were on the average more experienced, had longer tenure in their schools, and felt more committed to stay compared to the Maryland teachers (even though mean differences for commitment were not statistically significant). Kentucky and Maryland teachers rated their skill level and professional quality similarly, but Kentucky teachers had graver doubts about having control over the performance situation. Thus, the motivational pattern of mild pressure, low meaningfulness of accountability, high sense of competence, and low control over the performance situation applied to teachers in both states.

Teachers and administrators stressed continuity of their school's efforts to improve regardless of the school's status. Although public stigma hurt and instilled in most teachers a desire to shed the "in-decline" label, they reported to a lesser degree than Maryland teachers having exerted more effort as a result of probation. Thus, probation in the Kentucky schools was an altogether less stirring affair than in some of the Maryland schools. (This was 1998–2000, when the first wave of accountability demands was spent and the system was in the throes of political debate.) The majority of teachers indicated that they were committed to staying at their school regardless of its accountability status, notwithstanding probation being a prime reason for leaving the school and a cause for apprehension.

Less Organizational Rigidity

Compared to Maryland respondents, Kentucky respondents gave their schools higher marks on organizational capacity. Faculties were seen as more skillful and collegial and principals as more supportive and less controlling. Indeed, faculties in the four schools were more stable than in the Maryland schools, and the distribution of various levels of work experience was fairly normal. Principals themselves did not feel threatened in their jobs based on test scores, and indeed their tenure was rather long, exceeding 10 years in some cases. Three of the four principals owed their long tenure to district administrations that the state accountability system largely bypassed and where district interventions were not as prominent. Hence, the urgency that fueled control strategies in the Maryland schools was largely absent in the four Kentucky schools. An exception to this administrative stability was found in one of the elementary school, which had been led by no fewer than six principals in the previous 6 years. Teachers at this school reported that this inconsistent leadership inhibited their successful reform efforts.

Compared to the Maryland schools, the burden of accountability was shared to a larger extent in the Kentucky schools. One reason was the existence of site-based councils. The law that inaugurated accountability also provided for the devolution of decision-making authority from districts to the school level. While the site council did not usurp the authority of the principal in any of the schools, it may have tempered the principals' tendency to respond to probation with managerial control and the tendency of districts to constrain schools' choices with external mandates.

The presence of distinguished educators/highly skilled educators (DE/HSEs) in the Kentucky schools further distributed leadership with regard to school improvement efforts, but their effect should not be overestimated. Teachers in the study's four schools found the HSEs helpful but not of central importance. While 22% of teachers in these schools reported having intense contact with their HSE and less than 5% claimed to have no contact whatsoever, only about a fifth of the survey respondents from the four Kentucky schools attributed to DE/HSEs a strong effect on their school's improvement.

In three of the four schools, the role of the DE/HSE was absorbed into the traditional hierarchy of schools despite their considerable legal authority. HSEs offered their services to teachers who volunteered to invite them into their classrooms. The HSEs treaded lightly to avoid overriding the leadership of the principal. Thus, rather than being authoritative improvement managers as envisioned by the law, the HSEs functioned more as added resources. Teachers described their role as similar to that of other external consultants.

The most common response of the four case study schools to being labeled "in decline" was the alignment of curricula with the state test and core curriculum, the practicing of test-specific skills, and the adoption and implementation of a large number of new programs. This was visible in the four case study schools and in the content of the 32 school improvement plans we analyzed. It was common for schools to make sure that students had practiced a certain number of open-response questions and writing prompts. But further direct control of classrooms, as described for the two moving Maryland schools, was absent. Because the faculties in the four Kentucky schools were fairly stable, there was more evidence of the cumulative effects of past improvement efforts. For example, in the interviews teachers were quite aware and knowledgeable about details of the state assessments.

When asked how their school responded to probation ("in decline"), principals and teachers in all four schools pointed to many new programs. Often supported by Title I funds (for which the four schools qualified due to high poverty levels), comprehensive school reform demonstration funds, or other external funding, the schools attracted new programs for the entire spectrum of their operation. Thus, probation intensified the search for new programs and participation in professional development activities. "You name it, we've tried it," as one principal termed it. Several HSEs bemoaned that schools lost focus with this approach and that it left (low) expectations and classroom routines largely unexamined.

School improvement plans were similar to the Maryland plans in demonstrating compliance with external goals and suggesting a plethora of improvement strategies but dissimilar in their focus on curriculum alignment and their emphasis on school-internal performance barriers. Judging from the interviews conducted in the four schools, the DE/HSE played the explicit role of helping schools analyze their specific shortcomings in the area of curriculum and instruction. In addition to the HSE, instructional guidance of the Kentucky accountability system was more thorough and prescriptive, compared to the Maryland system. Core curricula gave teachers orientation in curriculum alignment.

In summary, probation in the Kentucky schools was a less stirring affair. The schools were more stable in terms of personnel, internal capacity was perceived as higher, and teachers were more experienced. By comparison to the Maryland principals, principals in the four Kentucky schools felt under less pressure from their districts, tempering the urgency for them to make an increase in test scores the top priority. Less pressure, more organizational stability and capacity, and more school autonomy made control strategies a less prominent feature in the four Kentucky schools, compared to Maryland. The Kentucky accountability system captured teachers' hearts even less in the four schools, but it compensated with more instructional guidance and change agent support.

ORGANIZATIONAL DEVELOPMENT
AND PROBATION—A CONCLUSION

Low in capacity and credibility, inundated with new programmatic and managerial mandates, and surveilled by state and district monitors, the seven Maryland schools on probation faced a narrow menu from which they could choose their school improvement strategies. Beyond the pressures of the low-performance label, districts exerted influence on schools through providing additional resources in the form of funds and material; offering an array of professional development workshops; adopting benchmark assessment instruments; and mandating specific teaching behavior, new instructional programs, and comprehensive school reform models.

Embedded in these external constraints and supports, the internal change dynamic set in motion by probation was similar across the seven Maryland sites in some respects and different in others. School improvement was to a large degree a matter of determined principal management, additional resources for new specialist personnel and retraining efforts, and top-down enforcement of programs and strategies. Generally speaking, the base for internal, self-directed participation among regular classroom teachers was small. Teachers expressed willingness to contribute to the school's success, though they rarely volunteered with concrete suggestions for their own classrooms.

Probation did not trigger intense organizationwide conversations about goals, responsibilities, and shared expectations. Rather than treating probation as a crisis and opening channels of inquiry into solutions with broad faculty participation, administrators tended to mute the voices of outspoken critics who might question the legitimacy of the accountability system but whose ardor might also expose the school to honest self-evaluation. Accountability was accepted as a fact. The meaning and value of performance goals were not publicly deliberated in most schools. The principals stressed consensus and unity, and the teachers were willing to rally around their leader as long as they sensed tangible progress, particularly in the area of student discipline, order, and test preparedness. Teachers resisted crude managerial control, but they accepted increased control in schools where it was laced with traditional paternalism and concrete assistance. In most instances, learning about accountability was restricted to the principals and the support staff to whom many new functions associated with accountability and probation were delegated. Teacher learning took place primarily as skill (re)training.

These were not circumstances under which internal group accountability could flourish. Strong managerial control by the administration, low commitment among teachers, the instability of the faculty from year to year, and the low motivational power of the accountability system sapped the momentum for internal group accountability that probation might theoretically trigger. Rather, principals became conduits of external pressures and roused their schools with administrative control strategies. Improvement strategies chosen by the schools corresponded to this leadership pattern. Schools relied on external programs, sweeping standardization, easily surveillable behavior, surface compliance, and test-preparation schemes that tended to trivialize the conceptual complexity of performance-based pedagogy. The fate of these strategies depended on the authority and leadership style of principals and their interaction with the administrative team.

Our successful cases had higher (perceived) capacity, compared to the schools that floundered. To begin with, they had stronger leaders, in terms of both principal support and control. Faculty members had higher trust in their colleagues' skills, and instructional specialists were better able to guide action with skills in test diagnostics and curriculum design. Capacity building was seen as more effective, and the district was more forthcoming with new resources and support. But also, probation made teachers compliant, and traditional prerogatives of teachers' classroom autonomy were overcome through administrative power attached to specialists' instructional support.

In the more successful cases, increased rigidity was associated with more organizational effectiveness. Discipline tightened. More attention was paid to the state assessments. Classroom teachers were on guard. Career teachers and instructional specialists were roused to action and rallied around the principal. A curriculum was being followed. In the moving schools, instructional specialists intervened more closely in daily curriculum. Increased participation in staff development workshops may have increased the competence of teachers (especially novice ones). Some of the seven schools posted modest improvements in this way. But increased organizational rigidity exerted a price. Teachers were dissatisfied. Some resented the pressure and standardization, and many contemplated leaving even when the schools visibly improved. Commitment to stay was not higher in the moving schools compared to the stuck schools, but skepticism about the accountability system's value was even more widespread in the successful schools.

Organizations are made up of people who interrelate with each other in patterned ways. Formal rules, stability in leadership, workers' ability to fulfill their job descriptions, adherence by personnel to the unwritten norms of the group, and the efforts of the group to socialize new members help maintain the continuity of the organization and make deliberate and sustained change possible. Common to the seven Maryland schools was a fundamental organizational instability. High student mobility and high teacher and administrator turnover kept the organization in flux. Some teachers were so untrained they could not maintain basic discipline and implement even highly prescriptive programs. Training effects from professional development workshops were wiped out from year to year. Schools lost teachers in key testing grades, sometimes midyear. In some cases positions remained unfilled all year long. Midcareer teachers in particular turned their backs on these schools. Wider labor-market conditions impinged on schools districtwide, but internal conditions and the low-performance label also contributed to this instability. Some schools were severely overcrowded while others were in need of basic physical repairs, adding to a spirit of siege and tenuousness.

Yet, despite the overwhelming problem of teacher commitment and work satisfaction, none of the Maryland schools placed this problem at the center of their strategies. Rather, the urgency of high-stakes accountability and probation for administrators seemed to have preempted such a focus and suggested the necessity for increased pressure and control primarily in the area of test preparation and standardization of instruction. The stuck schools employed similar measures but were less able to marshal these forces in effective ways, either because external support was lacking or internal leadership and capacity were missing. With schools lacking baseline stability, improvements either were not forthcoming or, when schools managed to improve, sustainability was highly uncertain.

Content analysis of school improvement plans and data from the seven Maryland schools testify to the state's success in involving schools and districts in the compilation of impressive, largely standardized documents that strongly reflected the state's model of school change. Most likely, this involvement did not extend to the large majority of regular classroom teachers, but it forced the most active parts of the teaching force—administrators and career teachers with special assignments—to apply the state's lens to their problem of low performance and, at the very least, to symbolically align their own view of change with the state's program. Despite widespread complaints, the SIP gave plan writers occasion for a thorough learning experience, an exercise in aligning their mental models (Senge, 1990) with the thinking of the state department of education. In the more passive parts of the teaching force, the SIP produced compliance that was at times stultifying.

The role of improvement plans in the internal development of the schools is less clear. At best, they seem to have functioned as an officially sanctioned lever that site administrators could use to demand unified action from faculties. In our sample of seven schools, this happened only when the principal backed the plan with a thorough internal monitoring system. Otherwise, the plan was widely ignored. Considering the enormous time and energy that was spent on compiling the plans, they were, at worst, an albatross that distracted educators from the business of actually making schools better. Planning in the Maryland schools on probation demonstrates both the penetrating power of accountability systems in eliciting obligations to external demands through managerial models of change and their limitations in bringing forth broadly based internal development.

Probation in the Kentucky schools was a less stirring affair. The schools were more stable in terms of personnel, and teachers were more experienced. By comparison to the Maryland principals, principals in the four Kentucky schools felt under less pressure from their districts, tempering their urgency about increasing test scores. Less pressure, more organizational stability, and more school autonomy made control strategies a less prominent feature in the four Kentucky schools.

In light of the Kentucky responses to high-stakes accountability, the rigidity effects detected in the Maryland case may not be a general pattern of response to probation. Instead, they may be related to a specific constellation of factors: more district control, threatened principals, and ordinary teachers with low skills, low commitment, and modest work motivation all working within a state accountability system that steers local districts with pedagogically complex outcome demands without a strong instructional guidance system and capacity-building strategies. Thus, one might say that the Maryland schools were a case of high administrative pressure meeting low organizational capacity. In the four Kentucky schools, we observed a more traditional pattern of school improvement through curricular alignment and accelerated adoption of new programs. The 11 schools had in common, however, an absence of dialogue about teachers' responsibility and the school's expectations and an absence of conversation about a meaningful response crafted in the tension between the school's and the accountability system's shortcomings.

PART III

Probation in Classrooms

ORGANIZATIONAL AND INDIVIDUAL LEARNING are key in accountability systems that aim at both higher intensity (Hargreaves, 1994) and more complexity in teaching and learning (Firestone, 1996; Knapp, 1997). In either of the two accountability systems studied here, schools, in order to master probation successfully, need to compel students not only to work harder but also to learn differently. Higher work intensity and tighter lesson plans—but also higher-order thinking, teamwork, verbalization, metacognition, deliberation, and reflective writing—are paramount.

The literature on teacher learning and knowledge (Shulman, 1987) shows that what teachers learn from policy depends on a host of factors: their extant practices; their understanding and interpretation of the policy; their own experiences, dispositions, and skills; and the support they receive in efforts to change their practices (Cohen, McLaughlin, & Talbert, 1993; Darling-Hammond, 1997; Grant, 1998). Grant's (1998) study of Michigan teachers attempting to incorporate instructional reforms found that teachers responded quite differently to the same reform, even though they were exposed to similar information about the intent of the reform and were given common direction on the use of instructional materials that were adopted by their school districts.

Teachers often do not see how policy demands for complex instructional change challenge their past practices and, therefore, do not see a need to learn new methods or change extant practices. Rather, they trivialize complex tasks to simpler task demands (Cohen, 1990; Spillane & Jennings, 1997). Spillane and Jennings (1997) show that when districts employed curriculum alignment strategies to change instructional practice, they often achieved superficial task modification but did not reach more deeply ingrained task and discourse structures in classrooms. For these to be changed, more intense and sustained learning opportunities are key.

Teachers weigh institutional demands, such as accountability goals, against the perceived needs of their students. When demands are ambitious and gaps are perceived as wide, teachers are more likely to question the relevance of the high standards for their students (Darling-Hammond & Wise, 1985). Perceived student needs exert strong pressures on teachers to adapt instruction to a level "that works" with *their* students. Often, teachers do not learn from the gap between high external performance demands and their level of instruction. Client needs and authoritative institutional demands are both accepted in their legitimacy and juxtaposed. Conflicts between them are left largely unexamined (Mintrop, 1999).

When probation is accompanied by managerial controls, as is often the case, administrators monitor teachers with increased record-keeping and standardizing surface routines that symbolize compliance but often decrease time for substantive work on lessons and professional collaboration (Cohen & Ball, 1999; Darling-Hammond, 1997). If teachers learn ambitious pedagogy through "revisiting and reinventing" (Cohen & Ball, 1999), then probation cannot succeed without accountability being connected to personal educational meanings and processes of organizational learning that facilitate exploring these meanings. But, as we saw previously, probation was particularly weak in facilitating such conditions. In the following chapter, we explore what kinds of instructional changes teachers attempted and enacted under these conditions.

CHAPTER 7

Instructional Change

WITH DARIA BUESE

CLASSROOM VISITS HELPED US UNDERSTAND how teachers taught, reflected on their teaching, interpreted the pedagogical demands of the performance-based assessments, and coped with the presumed gap between the high demands of the accountability system and the reality of their students' performance. We wondered whether the observed teaching matched the complexity of the state assessments and whether it justified the pervasive high sense of competence that teachers exhibited in surveys and interviews. A key function of accountability systems is to communicate to teachers expectations of high performance and to counteract presumed habitually deflated expectations of students in the low-performing schools. But teachers cannot learn from their shortcomings if they are not aware of them and if the necessary changes are not at least within their own reflective horizon (Hargreaves & Fullan, 1992). Teachers may have their own interpretation of the presumed performance gap and their own way of coping with it.

Recall that large numbers of teachers in the case study schools viewed themselves as highly competent professionals whose skills and knowledge measured up to the demands of the states' performance-based assessments. But at the same time, many teachers did not treat these assessments as gauges of their own performance and quality. Performance shortcomings were attributed mainly to factors over which teachers had little personal control. On the organizational level, probation in these schools was associated with a strengthening of organizational hierarchy and rigidity rather than internal dialogue and organizational learning. As a result, conversations about performance goals, student learning, and internal curricular changes were only weakly developed. External programs, surface control on the part of principals, and, in the more successful cases, intervention by instructional specialists were prevalent strategies. Moreover, while the state demanded an upgrading of teaching quality, in reality the schools struggled with high teacher turnover, low job commitment, and an increasing number of non-certified and inexperienced teachers. This is the situation in which we conducted classroom observations and engaged teachers in conversations about their classes.

Typically, we would visit teachers in their classrooms, observe a lesson, and then follow up with a debriefing interview. During these debriefings, observers had the opportunity to cross-check their interpretation of the lesson with that of the teacher and inquire how teachers reflected on the lessons' strengths and weaknesses and, especially, how they made the connection to accountability demands and perceived student needs. Lessons were usually observed by two observers to increase reliability of ratings. The two observers noted the sequence of the lesson and took so-called snapshots five times over the course of the lesson. During these snapshots, observers recorded what occurred at this particular moment in time and rated occurrences according to a prepared rubric.

STRUCTURE OF OBSERVED LESSONS

In the Maryland schools we visited 50 classrooms. After dropping from the analysis lessons for which we could not complete the full sequence of observation and debriefing, we ended up with the 30 lessons and debriefing interviews on which this chapter relies. We distinguish lessons according to two levels: basic and elaborate. Good lessons on the basic level are coherent, vary material and forms of interaction, stress simple content or cognitive skills, and employ teacher-centered forms of dialogue that engage students willing to learn. In elaborate lessons, students apply knowledge, generalize from examples, deliberate ideas, solve problems, evaluate answers, reflect on process, and engage in more complex forms of dialogue with fellow students.

Observation frequencies (see Table 7.1) show that teachers for the most part conducted lessons on the basic level. The frequency of higher-order thinking, problem solving, and complex dialogue among the counted snapshots during each lesson was very low. Between 70% and 80% of the lessons did not show evidence of elaborate-level teaching at all. Connections to students' experiences occurred more often, although over half of the lessons did not contain such an element of real-life application. More complex instructional methods, such as group or partner work, were evident, though 60% of the lessons did not contain such formats at all. In sum, if complex performance-based pedagogy is the basis for student success on the state assessment (in this case the MSPAP), these lessons fell short for the most part. In all likelihood, teachers' voluntary participation in the study excluded the worst examples of incompetent teaching from our observations.

On the basic level, lessons were more adequate. There was evidence of simple cognitive skills or content being learned in almost all lessons. In half

Table 7.1. Patterns of Instruction in Maryland Schools

Instructional Feature	Percent of Lessons [a]				
	4 or 5 Snapshots	3 Snapshots	2 Snapshots	1 Snapshot	Did Not Occur
Higher-order thinking	0	3	10	20	67
Problem solving	0	0	3	10	87
Dialogue complexity	0	0	3	13	84
Teamwork	3	7	13	17	60
Real-life application	7	0	17	23	53
Simple cognitive skills	50	27	7	16	0
Test drill	0	7	10	7	76

[a] $N = 30$.

the lessons this took place throughout. However, lack of conceptual depth was indicated by the large proportion of lessons that were not tightly held together by a common conceptual or topical threat. Only one-third of all observed lessons were deemed coherent; that is, the beginning, middle, and end hung together. On the positive side, teachers seemed to be skillful instructors as far as methods were concerned. In the overwhelming majority of lessons, teachers used a variety of materials, activities, and forms of interaction. In quite a few lessons variety was a very prevalent feature. Three or more activity changes occurred in 77% of all observed lessons and three or more changes in material in 47%. Interestingly, evidence of practicing simple test-taking skills was fairly low. "Drill and kill," as this test-driven instruction is sometimes called, was not observed at all in three-fourths of the lessons. It is quite possible that the complexity of the central performance-based assessment does not lend itself to the kind of narrowing of curriculum that has been found to accompany basic skills tests (Darling-Hammond, 1991; Noble & Smith, 1994).

In sum, the observed lessons exhibited a typical pattern. More complex forms of learning on the elaborate level were neglected. Many lessons lacked conceptual coherence, but learning on a basic conceptual level and instructional variety were widespread. Most lessons transpired in an orderly fashion or with occasional disruptions. The tone tended to be professional, and students, according to the raters, were either compliant or interested, in fairly equal proportions. Thus, conceptual depth and learning complexity were the most serious shortcomings, while instructional variety was a strong feature in the observed lessons.

CONVERSATIONS ABOUT TEACHING AND ACCOUNTABILITY

When we analyzed the relationship between patterns of teaching and ways of reflecting on practice and accountability, we discerned patterns that we capture in vignettes from eight teachers. Two of the teachers taught lessons classified as attempts to teach on an elaborate performance-based level, four are classified as solid on a basic level, and two are classified as marginal.

Elaborate-Level Lessons

Elaborate-level lessons were the most difficult to detect in our sample. They are better classified as attempts at meeting the complex nature of the state assessments. We observed five lessons that were attempts at this level. Two vignettes are presented here. One illustrates a lesson that was methodologically interesting but did not contain challenging difficulty of content. In the other, the teacher took up the challenge of performance-based pedagogy, guided by the official curriculum, but trivialized the constructivist nature of the exercise.

Ms. Knight. A teacher of English with 30 years of experience, Ms Knight, as a matter of routine, arranged her 26 eighth-grade students into groups of four or five. The lesson we observed was on writing practice. The lesson began with a playful warm-up activity. During the lesson, each group was given an abstract nonsensical picture. In their groups, students were asked to discuss their ideas about the pictures. After about 10 minutes, a bell rang and the students stopped their group work. Ms. Knight explained that they were to move apart and write paragraphs expressing their ideas about the pictures. For about 15 minutes the students, almost without exception, wrote intently. As the students worked, Ms. Knight circulated around the room, encouraging students to do their best work and prodding students who needed a little push. She admonished students to refer to the MSPAP writing rubric on the wall. Following seatwork, the students presented their paragraphs to the class; before dismissal, they were given a worksheet on MSPAP vocabulary.

    Ms. Knight's lesson objective was for students to "create a picture in their mind and then put it in writing, construct meaning from one place to another" (A-24). She was pleased with the lesson. Its strong point in her mind was that she was able to pique students' interest and creativity and to coax them to get up in front of the class and present their writing products. She was less certain about the intellectual depth of the lesson: "I think they could have written more in depth; in fact I know they could." As a remedy, she proposed extending the timeframe for the activity. She assured us that writing for fluency in reference to the MSPAP rubric qualified this lesson as a "MSPAP lesson," although the rubric itself was never directly used during the lesson for actual writing instruction. The observation took place 2 weeks before the test, so preparation for the test was intense: "Their homework is for MSPAP vocabulary. The closer we get, the more intense it becomes, but basically we try to incorporate MSPAP-type activities from day 1. And then the closer we get we just lay it on."

Probation, said Ms. Knight, helped her improve her teaching by tightening up her classroom:

> We are now held to certain standards and expectations, such as we have expectations for the students, the principal has some and administration has expectations for us and she checks to make sure that these things are being done. . . . In the past we've more or less been left to our own task and like I used to be guilty of not writing lesson plans. I'd come in, I knew what I wanted to teach. . . . Now she's called us in several times in staff meetings and you must write your lesson plans, so I have a stack of them over there on my desk. (A-24)

But at the same time, writing out lesson plans had little impact in her classroom. In her mind, her teaching style and the stock of lessons from which she drew did not change even though accountability had increased her principal's classroom supervision:

> Really, the only thing I do differently now is write out. . . . But other than that, there's nothing . . . that I've changed. I still have my objectives, my outcomes, my warm-ups. . . . That was all there before. (A-24)

Ms. Knight accepted the Maryland accountability system and wholeheartedly supported attempts to raise the test scores in her school. On the school's chances of success she commented, "I'm hoping, because we really put a lot of effort in this, that we will see an increase." But at the same time, she was not sure:

> We have students who come in here with a lot of baggage, some of it we have not gotten through yet. But yet we're expected to prepare them to make these wonderful scores on tests and I think we're just not equipped no matter how unique plans we have in place, and we have some darn good plans in place and they are in force this year. (A-24)

Ms. Peyton. A middle-aged African American teacher, Ms. Peyton had been teaching math for 15 of her 25 years in the classroom. She was, however, teaching the observed lesson for the first time. It came from one of the six mathematics series that were piloted in the school that year. Ms. Peyton taught it as instructed in the teachers' manual.

At the beginning of the class, the 18 eighth-grade students present were directed to do a short warm-up drill that was unrelated to the main body of the lesson, but beginning lessons with a warm-up was a required part of the daily routine. When the students finished—within about 10 minutes—they split into the work groups that had been established 2 days earlier and resumed measuring the circumference and diameter of different-sized circular objects. Ms. Peyton did not review the previous 2 days, nor did she introduce the present task. As students measured, they recorded their data on graphs for subsequent analysis. It took the entire period for the students to complete their measuring and graphing. Throughout the lesson, Ms. Peyton moved about the room, consulting with students and monitoring their progress. Toward the end of the period, she instructed students to stop what they were doing and proceeded to give a minilecture on the relationship between circumference and diameter. Her last announcement of the class period was, "There is a relationship and it is pi" (Field notes, G-16).

In the debriefing, Ms. Peyton told us that creating situations that primed students to make meaning out of abstract concepts was more time-consuming than she was accustomed to. She thought this lesson would take two class periods, but it had already consumed a third, she lamented. In previous years she had taught lessons strictly on a basic level. "I'm a math teacher," she said, "I'm used to, you know, this is this and this is this." But this lesson was more "MSPAP-like." Her objective was "to try and get them to be responsible in groups, so when they do the MSPAP they can sort of stay focused. And we've done measurements before like that but never having them link them together and find the relationship." Ms. Peyton, however, did not mention in her reflection on the lesson that she was the one who had explained the relationship; her students did not find it. What counted for Ms. Peyton was that students had the opportunity to work in groups and be involved in an activity; actively constructing the concept did not seem the paramount concern.

Ms. Peyton was open to trying new ways of MSPAP teaching. Her view of the textbook, the source of the observed lesson, was very positive:

> I love the book. I like the way they have it set up because in the
> teacher's manual . . . they match the skills in the book. First of all, it's
> set up by themes and they match the skills that are in that theme with
> the national standards. So it really is very close because I know the

MSPAP is taken from the state standards that they get from the national standards. (G-16)

Ms. Peyton believed the use of this textbook was a step on the road to improved MSPAP scores. "I know this approach in this book is what [the school district] would like to go to because I know this is closer to what the standards are and closer to what will help the children pass the MSPAP," she said. However, she doubted that the students would be passing the test any time soon: "Some of the things are in place, but the children are not quite there yet." For her, the challenge in adopting the new curriculum in her class was one of management and activities, less so one of concepts.

Frustration replaced excitement as Ms. Peyton talked about other more administrative procedures she was to follow due to the school's probationary status. She was also required to meet in various teams three times a week, which for Ms. Peyton occurred during her daily planning period. These demands came at an emotional cost to her, and she expressed feeling demoralized and frustrated:

> The accountability is like treating you more like a child. . . . I can understand how it is, and I can go along with it, but it certainly doesn't make me feel good about the fact that I have to do this. . . . So, I see it as the work doubling, and there are more things that we have to do and some of them I don't understand as to why it has to be that way. . . . I find it to be a little more frustrating as far as I am concerned and I think as far as the experienced teachers are concerned. And we do it, I mean, you know, they say "this" and we do it. The morale doesn't work very well. . . . The situation is more strained and you feel . . . like, if you don't do the right thing, then you're going to be punished. (G-16)

Basic-Level Lessons

The majority of the lessons in our study were taught at a basic level. They emphasized basic cognitive skills, presented a topic in a coherent way, and reached their audience. We selected four solid basic-level lessons taught by teachers recognized as effective at their schools. These four teachers represent four different ways of dealing with accountability. One teacher shifted lesson formats according to the specifics of each test, one teacher evaded the tests, one rejected aspects of the assessments that she considered too demanding, and one believed that following a district-adopted program would do the job. These four teachers were the backbones of instruction at their schools, known to run classrooms in which students were under control and learned something.

Ms. Hillman. A young African American woman in her third year at the school, Ms. Hillman taught a seventh-grade math lesson on the prime factorization of composite numbers. She began the lesson with a warm-up drill that reviewed the rules of divisibility for the numbers 1 through 10 with special attention to 3 and 4. Unlike in many other observed lessons, the content of the warm-up—the divisibility rules—was taken up again later in the lesson. A skilled classroom manager with 9 years of teaching experience, Ms. Hillman used her time efficiently, listing vocabulary relevant to the lesson on the chalkboard while the students completed their drill. As the students finished the drill, they were directed to copy the vocabulary words into their notebooks. Meanwhile, the teacher passed out calculators to the students. The quick, steady pace of the lesson compelled almost all the students to stay on task, and most were able to complete the warm-up drill and vocabulary task by the time Ms. Hillman called on the class to give her their attention.

Ms. Hillman drew two factor trees for a composite number on the chalkboard. While she did this, she incorporated the vocabulary words the students had copied from the board into her brief lecture. She spent a few minutes asking direct questions about factoring and called for volunteers to come to the board to create trees for two different numbers. While the volunteers were at the board, Ms. Hillman prompted the seated students to make observations about the examples being demonstrated. The rules of divisibility from the warm-up were brought up and when the teacher was satisfied that the students understood the concept of factorization, she assigned problems from the textbook for students to do individually at their seats. The students worked quietly for another 15 minutes. With 5 minutes remaining in the period, those who were not finished were instructed to complete the problems for homework. Then Ms. Hillman asked several students to make verbal summations of the work they had done that day. She stressed important points made by one of the students and handed out additional homework before the students left the room.

Ms. Hillman explained to us that she planned her lessons throughout the schoolyear around a combination of district curricular requirements and the state assessments, the MFT and the MSPAP. MFT skills were practiced twice a week. She noted a distinction between test-preparation lessons and "regular" curriculum-specific lessons. "If it's not Maryland Functional or MSPAP related—because we do have tasks that we can pull in— . . . if it's just a regular lesson, no MSPAP, no Functional per se, then I rely on the book" (B-17). She acknowledged that the lesson we observed was taught on a basic level and did not contain the components of a performance-based lesson:

> Well, nothing was performance-based. Today's lesson was more of a
> Functional skill than a MSPAP skill. They didn't really have a task,

you know, cooperative—MSPAP is cooperative. And it was nothing today that really relied on a cooperative style. So, it was more a Functional than a MSPAP today. (B-17)

For Ms. Hillman, each test represented a particular activity format. She identified the MSPAP with cooperative group work.

She believed it was her duty to raise student achievement even though she was aware that many of her students were not working at the cognitive level needed to meet the achievement expectations of the accountability system. She welcomed visitors in her classroom and did not mind the principal's regular checkups, for she was eager to learn, as she explained. She embraced the state's quest for higher test scores and was willing to shape her instruction to the various tests, but in the tangle between the state's expectations of high performance and the reality of her students' skills, her teaching was firmly anchored in her students' needs. Asked how she dealt with the wide performance gap, she said:

Well, one day at a time, basically. I know that the gap cannot be tightened within a short period of time. . . . And one class at a time as well, because a lot of times what I have planned cannot be done for each class. So, I have to modify. . . . So, I'm thinking, just, basically, go where the students are, and bring them up. . . . Start where they are, and then bring them up, and in time, if instruction is, if you're doing what you're supposed to do, then the scores will come up. (B-17)

Mr. Warner. An African American science teacher in his mid-forties, Mr. Warner came to teaching after having been in the military and running a business. The physical order of his classroom demonstrated his habit of approaching school life in a self-described businesslike manner. The classroom exuded order. Behavioral expectations were prominently displayed on posters around the room, and it was apparent from the respectful and attentive behavior of his eighth-grade students that they had assimilated the posted directives well.

We observed Mr. Warner teach a lesson on different forms of energy (mechanical, chemical, etc.) and the relationship between potential and kinetic energy. The lesson began with a routine warm-up that was on the chalkboard when the students entered the room. They were to write down one form of energy and list situations in which it was converted from one form to another. When the students completed their lists, several were called to the front of the room to present their work. There were many volunteers.

The lesson then moved into an examination of seven types of energy. The class read silently while one student read aloud from the textbook she was sharing. (There were not enough books for every student.) Mr. Warner stopped the reading repeatedly to ask students to give real-life examples of the energy conversions that were presented in the text, and students actively competed for the opportunity to supply answers. The concepts that Mr. Warner wanted reinforced were repeated several times, in the text that was read and in his questions. The lesson proceeded in this manner for about half an hour and ended with Mr. Warner's summation of the various forms of energy covered during the lesson.

Mr. Warner was very firm on the right way to teach the curriculum. He did not use the prescribed instructional program because "they don't break the concepts down the way I want them to be broken down." In reference to the adopted textbook he said, "I do a lot of work from other texts, and I use that [the adopted text] as the guidelines, since that is the text the county prescribes for us." Mr. Warner explained that he used the old science book with students "because this particular book [will] . . . teach a concept and then it will repeat the concept again."

Though there was no indication of a cooperative learning setup in the observed lesson, Mr. Warner said he employed a considerable repertoire of teaching techniques. "I use different types of teaching strategies. I use a lot of experiential learning with the class, and they tend to relate well to that." The lesson we observed, however, was very traditional. It was to prepare the students for an experiential lesson. He gave us a preview: "We'll probably do a sit-down tug-of-war where weight won't be a factor, and basically it will be power and strength. So that will be chemical energy and mechanical energy."

Mr. Warner was very open in relating his beliefs about teaching and learning, but he did not appear to be concerned about the state's accountability system. We pressed him to tell us how his lesson prepared students for the MSPAP, but his responses were evasive. He was doing what he thought was working best with his students, and he felt he was successful. Adopted curricula, accountability goals, and pressures faded into the background. He put it this way: "I would say that I'm somewhat of a risk taker and I'm always proactive toward the students. I'm always looking for avenues that will make my lessons more interesting, more expeditionary, and more experiential. . . . I'm the one that teaches the lesson." (A-25)

Ms. Clement. An African American with roots in her students' community and with 24 years of teaching experience, Ms. Clement ran a very organized classroom, and students were very disciplined when they were in her room. As a former union representative in the school for 5 years, she was an unofficial teacher leader at her site. She characterized her classroom with these words:

I'm borderline regimented, because I say, I run this classroom as a work station. It's a work cycle. I'm the supervisor, OK? Let's face it, schools are a business. . . . I'm, "What's the work plan here?" It's the written curriculum. That's what I'm paid to deliver, and I insist on doing that. (A-22)

She developed a structure that worked for her and her students:

I don't change it. I think back to what increases my students' comfort level. No matter what happens, I don't change, and they depend on it. That's important to them. It's also a part of classroom climate. My expectations don't change for them. They know what to expect. (A-22)

We observed Ms. Clement teaching a traditional, basic skills–oriented math lesson to an eighth-grade "resource" class. It began with warm-up computation problems that students copied from the board. After about 10 minutes, Ms. Clement went over the problems even though the students were not done with their work. After showing them how to get the right answers, Ms. Clement instructed the students to turn to their books and began demonstrating ways to use the distributive property to solve equations. Ms. Clement gave the students a problem to try. After correcting it, she gave the students an assignment from the book, and they began working. Students did all work throughout the class individually. After a few minutes, Ms. Clement noted that the students were making a lot of mistakes, so she called the class to attention and demonstrated a few more problems. The process of teacher modeling/student practicing proceeded as she assigned another set of problems from the text.

After the lesson, she commented:

A lot of times, if I start a lesson, and I find that they aren't grasping, and I don't see the kind of comfort level I need to see, then I will go back. You know, I stop and go back, and try to bring in prior knowledge . . . because I find that with this group, you know, they're really short-term memory. You know, it's here today and it's gone tomorrow, if not this afternoon. (A-22)

Order, routine, clear expectations, and adapting lesson difficulty to the comfort level of the students were the ingredients of her effectiveness. She would teach the lesson again "pretty much the same . . . because I noticed at the end of the lesson, except for some of them, that it was beginning to click." Ms. Clement proudly presented her students' latest scores on the MFT, for which she had practiced with them intensely. Ms. Clement did not reject the

MSPAP entirely, but she was largely unaffected by it. Probation had little impact on her classroom. Asked if she had changed her instruction since probation, she answered:

> No. I really don't, because the status of the school just put us on alert. But it didn't change . . . I have always felt that I've always been a committed teacher. . . . So, nothing really changed. My expectations certainly never changed. I have certainly been receptive to the information. . . . And regardless to how I feel about the MSPAP, my personal feelings, I don't bring that into my classroom. (A-22)

But with her characteristic outspokenness, she confided that ever since the school had become reconstitution-eligible, she felt under all kinds of conflicting pressures to rearrange instructional time and to cut back on basic skills development, which in her judgment was essential for her students. Two different types of tests, a district curriculum insufficiently aligned yet made absolutely mandatory, external monitors with specific expectations, a school administration veering between compliance and the school's self-interests, district and school subject-matter departments at odds with each other, and the perceived learning needs of the students being at odds with performance demands of the system—these were the cross-currents in which Ms. Clement upheld the structure of her classroom. She related:

> Prior to this year, we have always been allowed to pretty much, almost in isolation, teach the Maryland Functional skills to our students. . . . But we were told we have to dive into our curriculum because we had state people coming in and out of the building, and they're going to be looking for certain things, and they need to come in and find us working on a curriculum. Now I, on the other hand, know that if we are reconstitution-eligible, somebody's also going to be looking at our scores. I also know that when those test scores come back, I have the accountability for how many of my students pass that Maryland Functional Math test, which is a requirement for graduation. Now, this is what we were told by the master teacher: "If you follow the curriculum, the scope and sequence, those skills will be covered." No such thing. Not for eighth grade. . . . The scope and sequence which is supposed to be visible on our desk at all times [does not cover the functional test] . . . It was just not there. Now, I taught those [functional skills] anyway. I just decided, if someone comes in, and they want to address it, including [the principal] herself, then I was going to present my position to her. (A-22)

To Ms. Clement, the performance-based MSPAP was of lesser relevance: "I don't know if you want this on tape, but I have a sticker on my car that says, 'Stop MSPAP, teach basics.'" Though she "love[d] the performance assessment activities," she believed that "they would be better geared for our students who are more academically inclined, but for my students who are still stuck on the basics, I say this: I have a problem with trying to teach the Pythagorean theorem to students who can't do basic computation." For her, there was "too big of a gap" between MSPAP and what her students were able to do, "and I don't have to tell you our kids are usually just frustrated by the test."

Ms. Seegars. Reading proficiency is a priority in the primary grades. In one of the elementary schools, the *Open Court* reading series had recently been adopted to raise reading achievement. The lesson described here was taught by first-grade teacher, Ms. Seegars, a European American woman in her late thirties who had been in the school for 9 years. She was originally hired as the technology specialist at the school, but because of staffing problems midyear, she was placed in this first-grade classroom.

When we entered Ms. Seegars's room, the students were seated on the floor in a cluster reviewing the previous day's lesson. After a few minutes, they moved into a circle and began playing a game designed to help them practice the aural identification of long and short vowel sounds. After about 10 minutes, the students moved into another arrangement for a new activity. Ms. Seegars showed the students a card with a word or a sound blend on it, and the students chorally said the word or blend aloud. The students then returned to their seats, where they were directed to begin a handwriting activity. The lesson ended with a story circle. The teacher modeled silent reading for the students by reading a few lines quietly to herself, using her finger to track the words as she read. She then read the story aloud and led a short discussion about the rhyming words embedded in the text.

Nothing about this lesson was of Ms. Seegars's own design. It was coherent, sequential, and contained a variety of activities, interactions, and materials. Ms. Seegars's professional manner, firm tone, and steady pacing created an orderly climate in which almost all of the students displayed interest throughout the duration of our observation. In Ms. Seegars's view, the *Open Court* series encouraged this kind of teaching. "I'm very comfortable with the program," she commented. "It's a very typical lesson—it's scripted—it goes top to bottom. You just read the next thing on the page and go along and do it. . . . It takes the burden off of me."

Ms. Seegars described how *Open Court* representatives came into her classroom with a checklist, "to make sure you're doing everything you're supposed to do." She accepted these observations as a component of her professional development but noted that strict adherence to the program resulted in a lack of flexibility that made it difficult to teach an entire lesson in the language arts period of the day. Ms. Seegars said she got around this by stealing time from other subject areas: "When I go back after lunch, even though I'm not supposed to, I have to finish up my *Open Court*. But I like it so much that I'm willing to sacrifice a little time out of everything else." Acknowledging that this attention to reading skills cut into time for other activities, Ms. Seegars asserted that if her students were ever going to be successful on the MSPAP, "they have to be able to read the test. So that's my main focus now, because I think we were losing a little sight of the fact, that is they have to read." Ms. Seegars did not feel undue pressure as a result of teaching in a reconstitution-eligible school. For her, the new program would surely do the job of bridging the gap between her students' performance and the expectations of the accountability system, but she was worried that her colleagues were overtaxed with the implementation of the program, a worry that was confirmed by our observations in other classrooms.

Marginal Lessons

In marginal lessons we find little coherence among lesson components and there is infrequent evidence of simple cognitive skills being taught. This applies directly to about one-fourth of all observed lessons, though more lessons (47%) were observed to have breaks in their conceptual thread. The two teachers described below represent the relatively large numbers of young and inexperienced teachers working in the focal Maryland schools.

Mr. Carrother. This was Mr. Carrother's third year of teaching, his first as a middle school language arts teacher. His seventh- and eighth-grade students took their time entering his classroom. Many were late, not arriving until 5 minutes after the start of class. The usual warm-up drill was waiting for them on the chalkboard, but most sat down and immediately began conversing with their friends. One or two slumped down in their seats or put their heads on their desks to catch a few winks. Mr. Carrother was called into the hall by another teacher. Upon his harried return, now a full 10 minutes into the class, he called the students to attention and began the day's lesson on the classification of verbs. The objective was to distinguish between different types of verbs. He gave several examples of verbs in the different classifications, but his students—the few who were paying attention—looked puzzled and confused by his explanations. Private conversations multiplied when the teacher was sidetracked by one student who challenged him on contradictory remarks.

Called to attention again, the students were told to copy five sentences that were written on the chalkboard. They were to identify and classify the verbs in each one. Again, Mr. Carrother's instructions were unclear and the students who intended to do the assignment debated about what it was they were supposed to do. The rest continued their conversations, returned their heads to their desks, or did something altogether unrelated to the assignment.

In the debriefing, Mr. Carrother asserted that the students "were able to identify the verb for the most part. Sometimes, some of them weren't, but I would say maybe about 60% of them were able to identify it at least four out of five times" (G-21). When asked about MSPAP activities in his classroom, he assured us that "I can be rather creative when I'm in the right environment," but there were many factors, in his eyes, that were working against his creative potential: "I think that the whole concept of cooperative learning and collaborative learning is set up for the ideal environment, and it doesn't take into account for when a majority of students are bringing things from outside of the school that impact upon their learning [and] have a negative effect on the quality" (G-21).

As a relatively inexperienced teacher in a new school, he received little support. On his first day of school, his orientation to the school consisted only of being shown to his room and given a set of books. We asked him to describe what kind of help he received. "None. None," he said, "We're talking professionally, none. Deal with it. . . . There's no formal system of mentoring." Exacerbating the problem was the overwhelming amount of documentation teachers had to keep on students as a part of the school's accountability system. "We have to document everything that we do. Nobody ever reads the documentation. . . . but we have to document this, we have to document that. . . . We spend so much time documenting that now time is taken away from my lesson plan" (G-21).

Mr. Carrother had learned the difference between teacher-centered and performance-based activities from an education course he took; and because "we're told about MSPAP all the time," he knew that MSPAP was a performance-based assessment, but he was not sure MSPAP was appropriate for his students: "At some point I've got to say, 'You know what? Your MSPAP is nice but they need a knowledge base' " (G-21).

Mr. Carrother was clearly frustrated and perhaps even angry with his situation. When asked whether probation or the MSPAP influenced his teaching, he replied, "Is MSPAP driving what we're doing in any way? No. No. What's driving what we're doing is survival" (G-21).

Mr. Sinclair. In our final vignette, we enter the third-grade classroom of Mr. Sinclair. Mr. Sinclair, a young White teacher from Texas, entered the teaching profession through the Teach for America program. He was in his second of the 2 years of his teaching obligation. Mr. Sinclair's math lesson was intended to demonstrate how people use fractional units in their everyday lives. This was accomplished by taking the students on an imaginary trip to the grocery store. Mr. Sinclair explained that the change students received at the store could be thought of as a fraction of a dollar. After the pretend shopping trip, the students completed a worksheet, titled "A Trip to Safeway," that directed them to add up four dollar amounts in decimal form and then fill in a blank check converting decimals into fractions for the penny amounts.

The students were quite curious about the different aspects of the check, particularly the check number at the top-right-hand corner, and Mr. Sinclair had difficulty getting the students to focus on adding the dollar amounts and writing the check. The class slowly progressed to filling in the part of the check where the dollar amount was to be written out in words with the cents in fraction form. "How can money be thought of as a fraction?" Mr. Sinclair asked. He was faced by blank stares. Restating the question did not clear up students' confusion. After a few moments, a few students attempted to answer. Their answers made no sense. Mr. Sinclair again stated that cents could be thought of as fractions. More confusion ensued, and the students became restless. Now Mr. Sinclair was frustrated, and frustration turned into irritation. Eventually, he dismissed the question and moved on to the correction of the work students had done on the worksheet. It was now time for a bathroom break. To bring the lesson to some kind of closure, Mr. Sinclair quickly recapitulated the answers to the problems on the worksheet. As the students were dismissed to the restroom in small groups, Mr. Sinclair asked them what they had learned today. One student answered that people can change the numbers on the check to increase the amount (F-20, field notes).

In the debriefing, Mr. Sinclair commented that he didn't think "that a lot of the kids . . . were . . . able to explain how money can be converted to fractions" (F-20). Mr. Sinclair confessed that when he asked the question, he "was a bit confused at that point too." The decimal conversion question came "straight out of the curriculum," so it didn't occur to him how difficult the concept was for third graders. He was unaccustomed to questioning the curriculum because he trusted it to be conceptually coherent and grade-level appropriate. Though he estimated that only half of his students were on a third-grade level, he nonetheless used the third-grade curriculum as directed. Making modifications for the many students below grade level seemed difficult:

> I don't have direct access to second-grade books or anything in here. . . . We as teachers are expected to have these certain things covered by the end of the year. And having it broken down on a day-

by-day fashion lays out what we need to have done, in the scope and sequence kind of fashion. (F-20)

Being unconvinced of the attainability of success on the MSPAP, Mr. Sinclair was, in his words, "worn out" and "run down" by trying to reconcile the reality that "a lot of things that the kids come into school with are things that are way beyond my control" and being held accountable for student achievement. He intended to leave teaching at the end of the schoolyear.

INSTRUCTIONAL CHANGE AND PROBATION—A CONCLUSION

Taken together, the eight vignettes describe a variety of teachers with respect to teaching expertise, reflective capacity, and coping with the accountability system. They describe how teachers in schools on probation interpret their task in light of external performance expectations, their own internal standards, and the perceived needs of their students. Six of the eight teachers were seasoned teachers who ran effective classrooms. Two of the teachers were fairly new in their careers, overwhelmed by the situation, and only marginally effective with their students. Quantitatively, marginally effective teachers were more common in the seven schools than the selection of just two vignettes would suggest.

All of these teachers were acutely aware of the accountability system, not unlike the larger group of observed teachers whose voices and experiences are echoed in the eight vignettes. Most of the other teachers whose classrooms we visited and who talked to us considered it unlikely that their students would reach the lofty goals the accountability had set out for them. But they were willing to try concentrating on incremental learning steps. In negotiating the gap between external performance demands and the perceived abilities of their students, teachers primarily gauged their lessons to students. The desirability of performance-based tasks was overshadowed by the perceived necessity for basic skills development. Teachers felt justified teaching lessons in a format that traditionally "worked." Basic skills tests that are part of the accountability system in middle schools legitimized this view. Many seasoned teachers looked askance at the push for performance-based pedagogy.

In the view of many, MSPAP activities distinguished themselves mainly as writing activities, group work, and the use of particular analytic vocabulary. For fewer teachers, reflection on one's own thought process was also associated with MSPAP. This pattern holds across all observed teachers. Thus, the conceptual depth of knowledge construction was often simplified into a set of activity formats. Judging from the debriefing interviews that accompanied lesson observations, teachers were, for the most part, not aware of this task trivialization.

Although teachers strongly expressed the notion that their lessons were first and foremost adapted to their students' ability and achievement levels, tests, new instructional programs, new curricula, and new textbooks reached deeply into many teachers' classrooms, although external pressures and directions were multiple and often conflicting. Some teachers, like Ms. Hillman, believed that different kinds of assessments required different kinds of lessons. Many of the more compliant teachers felt obligated to teach the prescribed curricula, like Mr. Sinclair, regardless of the fact that they were not suitable for students below grade level. On the other hand, seasoned, self-confident teachers, such as Mr. Warner and Ms. Clement, learned to dodge the system and were quick to make adjustments when they felt it was appropriate. In the survey, more than half of the teachers had indicated that they were clearly directed by the accountability system. In the context of classrooms, this clarity appeared to be much more laden with conflict.

Adoption of new instructional programs and curricula was one way that districts attempted to improve probationary schools. In many cases, particularly in the elementary grades, teachers not only accepted their use but also appreciated their ease of use. Following scripted programs and teaching the official curriculum, lesson by lesson, was teachers' most frequent answer to our question about what they did to help their students be successful on the MSPAP. These programs and curricula created putative certainty in the uncertain performance situation. By following them, many interviewees felt they had fulfilled their obligations and thus assumed they were doing right by the accountability system. Many teachers, some of them described in the vignettes, professed to faithfully implement the programs, sometimes with little forethought. Scripted programs were deceptively easy, but they, too, required training and were too complicated for some teachers.

All schools had procedures that required teachers to have MSPAP rubrics on their walls, use MSPAP words of the week, write detailed lesson plans, or keep portfolios on students. The vast majority of teachers complied with these routines. However, the manner in which they were used varied from teacher to teacher. Some considered the extra duties a nuisance and an affront to their professionalism. Fewer viewed them as "good pressure."

For all their resentment, many teachers, almost in passing, expressed habitual compliance with administrative mandates intended to align instruction with MSPAP. Although they saw the accountability system as unhelpful and stacked against them, they did not reject it and did not outright condemn it. They truly served two masters. They wanted to concurrently accept the institutional weight of the state and be sensitive to the needs of their students, but the two pulled from opposite ends. Tensions were diffused in several ways. Mr. Warner and Ms. Clement discarded the state's directives by virtue of their unreasonableness or irrelevance. Others, like Mr. Carrother, discarded the students because they were, in his eyes, uneducable. But for the great majority, adopting officially sanctioned programs, curricula, and materials was the defensive retreat that relieved them of dissonance and delegated the decisions and responsibilities to a higher level. Teachers developed their own coping mechanisms in collective silence without collective debate and decision making at the school, but with a groudswell of dissatisfaction.

Teachers' assurances to the contrary, we saw a discrepancy between the way teachers taught and what was required to be successful on the state assessments. How can this discrepancy be explained? To begin with, only a few teachers took the gap between external performance expectation and internal performance reality as an occasion to learn. There was little awareness of how far off the mark these schools actually were in terms of teaching in ways appropriate to the assessments. The response of the majority was defensiveness or compliance. Many teachers trivialized performance-based pedagogy as a set of discrete activities. Willingness to follow directions and the presumed focus of accountability systems were undermined by mixed messages, conflicting demands from various decision makers, perceived inappropriateness of the central assessments for students, and lack of fit between mandated curricula and perceived student needs. Though new instructional programs were acceptable to many, cumbersome reporting and the putting up appearances of compliance that held sway in almost all schools turned them away from embracing probation as a serious matter that went to the core of their daily teaching.

Patterns of instruction in the small number of classrooms we visited in the Kentucky schools were very similar to the patterns encountered in the Maryland schools. Most lessons were taught on a basic level, some lessons were marginal, and elaborate lessons were a very infrequent occurrence.

During the 2 years of the study, the state of Kentucky scrapped the original performance-based test and replaced it with another test that reverted to more traditional testing formats. This test expanded portions with subject-matter-based multiple-choice questions and reduced the importance of portfolios and performance-based tasks. As a result, compared to the MSPAP in Maryland, the Kentucky test was more connected to prevalent instructional formats. A teacher in one of the elementary schools described her adjustment this way:

There was such an emphasis in hands-on things for several years that paper/pencils just completely went out the window. . . . Now I think

we've found a good mix of that and I think as a result of the testing
that made us . . . get more paper/pencil things back. (10-02; kindergarten teacher)

While Maryland teachers saw the tasks of the MSPAP as more generic and
less subject-matter-based, curriculum alignment and the concern for coverage was a unique concern for Kentucky teachers:

If we were told exactly what we should teach specifically, but we're
not. You're given opportunities to use trade books, various textbooks, and creative ideas, and then we're testing, and that range of
opportunity is so broad and the testing is so narrow that it's really
hard to hit everything they know . . . so I think it's a really difficult
way to look at the teacher and say that she has been accountable or
not. (30-5)

But most teachers said they tried to cover the core curriculum as best they
could:

Well, each school does an aligned curriculum, so that's what I'm
supposed to teach. That's my aspect of it. . . . What we try to do is
make sure that we have given them a thorough review for the test.
We try to get as much through as possible. With the test, they give
you roughly what percentages, like 10% is going to be weather and
stuff like that, so you say, "Well, OK, it's going to be 10% weather,
so I can give them worksheets on weather and give them a project on
weather." Things like that. (40-15; sixth-grade science teacher)

None of the Kentucky teachers we visited in their classrooms reported
instructional sea changes as a result of curricular alignment. Most teachers
described their instructional changes as "add[ing] skills here and there" (10-
10; second-grade math teacher), probation leaving the core of their teaching
unchanged. An eighth-grade English teacher reflected on these changes this
way:

I don't think I'm a better teacher because I'm in decline trying harder.
I think that if you're not a good teacher, you're not going to be a
good teacher no matter what. If you're a good teacher, that's the kind
of person that you are, that's what you care about. I do post stuff,
though, because I'm supposed to. . . . I didn't have all the nice little
things that they give us, so now I can label everything I do. . . . We
have to give an open-response question every 6 weeks and we have to

turn it in. Those kinds of things. We have to give information to people. We have to post these content standards. (40-16)

Judging from the Kentucky data, teachers in the four schools integrated assessment-specific skills and instructional formats (test vocabulary, portfolio, writing prompts) into their instruction, and they were striving to cover the topics of the state's core curriculum. Because of greater stability of faculties, Kentucky teachers were better informed and more sophisticated about their state's assessments. But at the same time, teachers felt fairly autonomous in their decisions to teach according to their best judgment and to select programs that suited their needs.

On the positive side, neither in the Maryland nor in the Kentucky classrooms did we encounter much of the mind-numbing test drill and practice that has been found to accompany accountability systems in which traditional basic skills tests have become high-stakes. But on the negative side, most observed teachers in both states did not translate ambitious external demands into high internal performance expectations that could foster a critical evaluation of one's teaching.

Excluding those many inexperienced teachers in the schools that struggled, at times helplessly, with basic teaching competencies, most of the more seasoned teachers whose classrooms we visited in either state might do well in an accountability system that called for more rigorous instruction in basic skills. Such a system would be more closely pegged to already existing teaching styles and performances. But the investigated accountability systems were more ambitious. They combined the press for more work effort with a demand for a new pedagogy. This change demands that teachers be motivated to learn and become proactive. In the observed classrooms, however, such learning was widely absent, and instructional change stalled.

CONCLUSION

The Potential and Limits of Sanctions

ACROSS THE UNITED STATES, high-stakes accountability policies that reward schools for good performance and penalize them for failing to maintain acceptable performance levels have proliferated. After disappointing results of earlier redistributive policies from the 1960s onward and attempts to mobilize the profession during the restructuring movement of the late 1980s, high-stakes accountability policies shifted reform emphasis from money or teacher empowerment to external standards, pressures, and incentives. Pressures are compounded for schools on probation because these schools are confronted with the stigma of the low-performance label, the threat of more severe penalties, and increasing oversight and scrutiny.

Within the spectrum of accountability systems across the United States, the Maryland and Kentucky systems were unique in their emphasis on performance-based assessments and their press for more complex instruction. Such systems require a higher level of internalizing accountability goals than systems based on simple basic skills assessments because changes in the instructional core involve a higher degree of learning and teachers' self-initiative. Such changes happen if accountability goals are meaningful and organizational conditions at the school are conducive to learning and problem solving.

The 11 schools on which we focused serve traditionally underprivileged student populations with high proportions of poor and minority students. These schools have the typical problems for these kinds of environments: high student mobility, discipline problems, lack of parental involvement, low overall achievement, lack of motivation to learn among students, irregular attendance, health and nutrition problems, and so on. Clearly, the schools are challenging work environments. Thus, in our study probation had to prove its worth under the challenging circumstances of ambitious state demands meeting hard cases. But this is in line with the policy talk that accompanies high-stakes accountability, in which probation comes across as a get-tough measure for persistently failing schools.

Primarily relying on external levers aimed at schools that are often in severe distress, high-stakes accountability policies need to be linked to schools and internalized into the beliefs and practices of school administrators and teachers. One link would be that educators work toward higher test scores because they desire to overcome the stigma of the low-performance status and are confident of being successful, perhaps reflected in such statements as, "We are better than it appears and we will prove it. Let's get those scores up." Another link would be an acceptance of external accountability goals as meaningful for one's own expectations, perhaps reflected in such statements as, "These goals are good goals and they are worth striving for, even if we don't succeed right away." A third link would be administrative pressure filtering down from top to bottom, coupled with an appeal to teachers' diffuse commitment to their leaders, colleagues, or students, perhaps reflected in such statements as, "I know we do not like this system, but we have no choice. Don't let your school down on this one" or, if administrative pressure is coupled with new resources, "Without probation we wouldn't have this new money. We can now do the things we always wanted to do and improve." Lastly, teachers comply with new instructional interventions (e.g. prescriptive programs, curriculum, instructional specialists) out of apprehension or fear about more severe penalties, perhaps reflected by the building principal statement, "Just follow the policies. It's time to shut up and shape up. Otherwise they'll be consequences that the state has in store for this school."

All these ways of linking were present in the 11 schools of the study. In the Maryland schools, the prevalent impetus was a mixture of administrators' appeal to teachers' commitment combined with pressure to comply with new interventions. In the Kentucky schools, diffuse commitment to the school and a desire to overcome the public stigma were stronger. Notably weak in all the schools was the belief in the meaningfulness of accountability standards for evaluating teachers' work. Across all the schools, responses varied according to the organizational capacity of the school.

PRESSURE, MEANING, AND CAPACITY

The low-performance label and the negative publicity that accompanied it came as a shock to some teachers, especially those with more seniority, but in time teachers distanced themselves from the system's verdict and reinterpreted it. The threat of the more severe sanctions tended to be discarded as not credible, and the label came to symbolize the school's neediness rather than educators' performance deficits. In the face of publicized failure, teachers reasserted their personal competence, mainly by externalizing causes for low test scores, but the label nevertheless hurt, and many wished to be rid of it. Not too many people at the schools embraced probation as good pressure. Those who did tended to be administrators or teachers in more administrative roles. Probation was not a threat but a nuisance, due to the public stigma that attached itself (in varying strengths) to these schools and due to the "fishbowl" atmosphere in which teachers carried out their daily duties after the school was "named."

Low commitment to stay at the negatively labeled school diminished the threatening nature of probation even further. Large proportions of teachers, particularly in the Maryland schools, were ready to leave their school. Probation was not always the stated reason for leaving, but it was indirectly responsible. Probation increased outside interference in classrooms, caused additional work pressure, and, for some teachers, reinforced a sense of doom for the school. In Kentucky, where job commitment was higher but exit options fewer, teachers cited escape from the label of probation as their prime reason for leaving their schools.

A majority of teachers found the attainment of higher test scores important, and an overwhelming number wanted to see their school shed the probation label, primarily out of concern for their professional reputation. Although some teachers, particularly senior teachers confident of their efficacy with challenging students, expressed defiance as they questioned the states' capacity to do the job better than teachers themselves, the states' rule-making authority was overwhelmingly accepted. Many voiced their willingness to comply and be directed by the accountability system in their instructional decisions, but not because the accountability system was seen as meaningful.

Whether one was an ordinary classroom teacher, teacher leader, or administrator, the systems were widely held to be unfair to teachers serving disadvantaged students, invalid as a gauge of teacher performance, and unrealistic in their expectations. Teachers were more prone to evaluate themselves based on observable behavior and reactions from students and other adults at school than based on the state's assessments. Personalization, incrementalism, and a basic skills orientation prevailed over a data-driven approach, ambitious growth targets, and performance-based pedagogy. Where the accountability system put the spotlight on a school's putative performance gap, teachers saw a gap between state demands and student needs. Thus, for the most part, educators in these schools derived meaning for their work from sources other than the accountability system. This is even more true for teachers (and moving schools in the aggregate) who reportedly exerted more work effort as a result of probation. These teachers tended to be even more skeptical about the accountability system. At the same time, teacher leaders were just as likely to move on as their less involved colleagues.

Thus, the two accountability systems largely failed to instill meaningful performance goals in educators in the studied schools on probation, and they failed even more miserably with the more active members of the profession. An incentive system that cannot appeal to the higher-performing parts of the workforce is doomed to failure. The systems insufficiently tapped into teachers' personal sense of responsibility for performance. As a result, school improvement for the majority was mainly externally induced and directed, prodded by administrators, instructional specialists, external consultants, staff developers, and so on whose activities were moderately fueled by a common desire among teachers to be rid of stigma and scrutiny and eased by a disposition to be compliant that the climate of high stakes fostered. Consequently probation primarily moved anxious administrators, mobilized career teachers, and helped external consultants to work on compliant teachers, whose commitment to the organization was often shaky.

All schools engaged in professional development, adopted mandated programs, and ran test-preparation schemes. But only in a few schools was the intervention fine-grained enough to reach daily instructional routines. None of the studied Maryland schools were able to unfreeze and engage in a process of internalizing accountability, that is, of finding meaning in the probationary status—a process that might have involved a personalized analysis of performance shortcomings and an active search for solutions that were meaningful and appropriately adapted to classroom realities as perceived by teachers. Administrative pressure was the default response that preempted processes of organizational learning. Across the Maryland schools, movement was achieved through determined management of the principal, who empowered instructional specialists to oversee implementation of instructional strategies. Many strategies were mandated by districts, and they were often packaged or standardized programs. School improvement plans also appeared to be written in response to external pressure. In the Kentucky schools, pressure was less emphasized, but the schools amassed a "war chest" of external programs and consultants that crowded out work on teacher performance expectations and key instructional routines.

Organizational capacity was a key factor in schools that moved as a result of probation. Principal leadership and faculty collegiality, as well as trust in the skills of colleagues, were perceived as stronger in those schools. The same was true on the individual level, where more motivated teachers also tended to see their schools as stronger organizations. In the interviews, educators mentioned "the faculty pulling together" as a key condition for their success in conjunction with the provision of external capacity building. Yet most of the studied schools, more so the ones in Maryland, suffered from low organizational capacity caused by high teacher turnover, inexperienced teachers, unfilled vacancies, weak principals, or high principal turnover.

It is the avowed strength of high-stakes accountability systems that the presence of standards and assessments coupled with the pressures of sanctions provide the impetus to focus on student achievement and instruction.

Teachers' own priorities for school improvement are different. In the question-naire, respondents were asked to indicate the 3 most critical areas for school improvement out of a list of 21. Improving student discipline and stabilizing teacher motivation and commitment to stay were considered by far more im-portant tasks than work on instructional methods or pedagogy. Thus, con-cern for social aspects of schooling prevailed over instructional ones (see Figure Conc. 1). System demands and teacher needs were incongruent. As account-ability systems called for student achievement, teachers answered back with an entreaty for baseline stabilization of their schools, needs that had less to do with teacher performance and more to do with organizational capacity.

In high-stakes accountability systems, systemic incentives (goals, sanc-tions, rewards) generalize the effects of accountability policies whereas local capacities particularize them. The effect of high-stakes accountability may be rather uneven across schools and districts, if the studied schools are any indication, because for them local capacity—that is, administrative control filtering from the top to the bottom of the bureaucratic hierarchy, internal organizational capacity, and external support—made a big difference. By

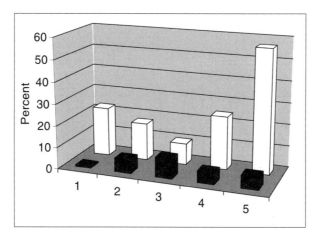

Figure Conc.1. Critical areas for school improvement perceived by teachers: Percent-age of respondents rating the area as critical. Black bars show curriculum and instruc-tion areas; white bars show social relationship areas. For curriculum and instruction areas, 1 indicates new pedagogical theory, 2 indicates child psychology, 3 indicates new instructional methods, 4 indicates performance-based pedagogy, and 5 indicates new instructional materials. For social relationship areas, 1 indicates motivation of teachers, 2 indicates stabilizing faculty turnover, 3 indicates the spirit of the school, 4 indicates respect for teachers, and 5 indicates student discipline.

contrast, systemic incentives had a dubious quality and were far less relevant. Accountability systems therefore are in need of a strong feature of capacity building that compensates for local differences.

DOES PROBATION WORK?

On the positive side, almost all of the 11 schools were modestly energized by the label, at least at some point or from time to time. Some teachers in all schools reported that they increased work effort and engagement in school improvement as a result of pressure and direction. Management in some schools tightened up; educators paid closer attention to the state assessments; support from instructional specialists or "highly skilled educators" intensified; and the adoption of new programs, strategies, and projects accelerated. In this way, a number of schools were able to remedy some inefficiencies and provide more structure to teachers than previously had been there. Considering rampant capacity deficits, they did it mainly through increasing control and standardization of teachers' classrooms. By remedying gross inefficiencies, many schools may be able to "harvest the low-hanging fruit," as my colleague Pat Martinez-Miller calls this stage, but they make few further inroads into the territory of instruction.

This may explain why in Maryland, statewide, schools with a record of deterioration showed a reversal of the worst decline at least initially; why the effect was not lasting and consistent; and why, for the majority of schools, probation had not spurred performance increases on the scale needed to lessen their tremendous performance lag in the medium term.

Had state assessments been less complex and more oriented toward basic skills, probation may have "worked" better; that is, the pressure of the stigma combined with various control strategies and program standardization could have produced an intensification of instruction based on already existing competencies and instructional formats. But even under these circumstances, pressure is a double-edged sword. It may challenge people to increase work effort but also make them want to leave if they do not see the pressure as serving a worthy purpose.

Probation was not working well as a tool for self-evaluation. Rather than accepting criteria and judgments of the system, teachers felt singled out as the ones who had to carry the "blame" for student learning and, in turn, externalized the causes for underperformance. Thus, instead of strengthening internal accountability in the 11 schools, high-stakes accountability triggered an unproductive blame shifting: the system placing responsibility squarely on educators' shoulders and educators, in turn, deflecting it back to society.

Probation did instill in schools the notion that "something" had to be done, but in none of the schools did the status trigger strong internal accountability, if this is to mean a process through which a faculty formulates its own expectations in light of student needs and high demands of the system, agrees on formal structures that hold them to account, and focuses improvement on identified key instructional deficiencies.

This kind of internalization process was neglected in the Kentucky schools but forestalled in the Maryland schools. The pattern of rigidity encountered in the latter is an example of what happens when high-performance demands and top-down pressure meet low-capacity schools. The result was a proliferation of control strategies that had the potential to turn classrooms into the opposite of what performance-based pedagogy intended. Being in the "fishbowl," most teachers tightened up traditional lesson structures. Coverage and task completion reigned supreme, and as token acknowledgment of the new pedagogy, more group work and writing assignments were added.

Looked at from the perspective of the seven focal schools, the Maryland case illustrates the limits of steering educational reform through incentives and sanctions derived from outcomes without an articulated capacity-building strategy that could have provided curricula, materials, and necessary teacher competencies as a bridge between high demands and perceived student needs. The state left capacity building largely in the hands of local districts, with the result that external demands and pressures fell upon wholly unprepared schools that reacted with rigidity rather than learning. Organizational rigidity may thus be related to a specific constellation of forces: more district control, threatened principals, and ordinary teachers with low skills, low commitment, and modest work motivation all working within a state accountability system that steers local districts with pedagogically complex outcome demands without providing the tools to reach them. In the Kentucky cases, these responses were avoided. Here, by contrast, higher-capacity schools responded to a system that was less ambitious pedagogically, more prescriptive as to curriculum, and more supportive through the highly skilled educator feature.

But there are success cases among the Maryland schools on probation as well. And one of the moving schools in our sample may give us an idea of what went into their improvement: an experienced principal, exceptional instructional specialists with data analysis, curriculum development, and coaching abilities, as well as additional resources provided by the district. And yet prospects for this school were dim. Without a process that involves all faculty members as responsible and committed actors, rather than mere implementers, and without a secure base of competent and committed teachers and administrators, the school may find itself at a loss again as key leaders exit.

The accountability systems in both states operate on the assumption of organizational stability. Only this assumption makes it legitimate to publicly expose putative deficiencies of whole schools based on year-to-year comparisons of schoolwide test scores. The reality of the studied schools on probation, however, was quite different. Some of the Maryland schools had almost complete personnel turnover between the time we began our study and the time we ended it. Some of the Kentucky schools saw a dramatic deterioration of their social indicators (e.g., students eligible for free or reduced-price lunches) while they declined. Performance trends and improvement continuities that accountability systems have constructed for whole organizations become fictitious under these circumstances. Improvement gains become tenuous and stable upward trends over time a rare occurrence. Under conditions of high organizational instability, continuous improvement is an elusive possibility.

If high-stakes policies were working properly, one would expect teachers with higher work motivation and teachers in moving schools to have higher job commitment and provide the kind of organizational continuity that a sustained improvement process requires. But this is not so, as we saw. Higher- and lower-motivated teachers, inexperienced teachers and teacher leaders—all were just as likely to leave their school, and they did so in large numbers. Thus, many of the schools needed baseline stabilization first before they could embark on ambitious instructional reforms. The actors responsible for this kind of stabilization are for the most part districts and states, not schools. But schools are the units of accountability in either system.

THE PERSISTENT PERFORMANCE GAP

The result was that in the majority of the studied schools, gaps between high state expectations and schools' reality persisted. Although majorities of teachers across the 11 schools stated that they had the requisite skills to teach according to the expectations of their accountability systems, classroom observations showed that teachers rarely taught according to these expectations. Many teachers' lessons were not adjusted to the pedagogy emphasized by the core assessments in either state. Higher-order thinking, problem solving, metacognition, extended dialogue, and so on were rare features in the observed lessons. In some classrooms, students were given the opportunity to write, to work in groups, and to make presentations, but often the scaffolding of cognitive processes was missing. While a number of lessons were solid on a basic level, many more lessons lacked coherence and quite a number were instructionally poor. Given the apparent gap between the external performance expectations of the state accountability systems and the instructional reality of observed classrooms, and given the additional pressure that probation lends to these external expectations, why is it that teachers take so little heed and why is it that so many of them believe that things are the best they can be as far as their own performance is concerned? In other words, why do the high-performance expectations of the accountability systems not provide greater challenges for teachers to make their instruction more intense and intellectually complex?

First of all, the assessments used by the states had little meaning for many teachers as adequate measurements of their own performance. Constructed on a cognitive level that resulted in large proportions of students failing year after year in these schools, the assessments were unconnected to the daily flow of instruction. The accountability system did not provide a bridge between the ideal of more cognitively complex and intellectually rigorous instruction and the perceived need to teach basic skills to the type of students teachers thought they faced in the low-performing schools.

Many teachers did not perceive the gap between their own instruction and that envisioned by the assessments in either state as all that wide. They believed they had in fact aligned their teaching to the demands of the system by having extended time for writing and group work, by drilling test vocabulary words and practicing test-specific writing formats, and by following district-adopted curricula and programs (in the case of Maryland) or attempting to cover as much of the state core curriculum as possible (in the case of Kentucky). For these teachers, the complex reform task demanded by state standards and assessments was interpreted as a more simplified incorporation of discrete instructional activities into their regular teaching style. For teachers who valued high test scores for primarily extrinsic reasons—that is, as a way to exit probation and not as a gauge of their own performance—such a short route to maximizing scores made sense. Patterns of leadership, organizational interactions, and improvement strategies were reflective of the same approach. For the most part, teachers were confronted with new programs and projects whose alignment with the assessments they accepted as an act of faith. They were asked to implement discrete and generic test-attack strategies, writing formats, and so on; were prodded to demonstrate compliance with instructional surface structures (e.g., warm-up phases, posting of test vocabulary and lesson objectives, table group seating); or were directed to align the content of their curriculum to the state's core content, no further questions permitted.

When students were under control, were on task, and seemed to have some comprehension of the lesson content, many teachers felt comfortable with their lesson. Keeping control of one's classroom, making students work, and directing their attention to the learning goals of the lesson were not givens in the environments of the 11 schools; quite the contrary, they entailed visible effort in many classrooms. The importance of the ambitious instructional and learning goals of the accountability system paled in the face of these daily challenges.

Thus, it was not that teachers rejected the ambitious accountability goals; rather, they were either not aware of the wide gap or, if they were aware of the gap, they did not know how to bridge it. Apparently, the existence of high external expectations coupled with the pressures of probation were not sufficient to bring about such awareness, knowledge, and capacity.

Absent was a process of internalization in which schools developed meaningful goals in light of real student work from the bottom up. In this process of school-internal accountability, state standards and realistic accountability goals would frame schools' own norms of performance and steps of improvement. If both official goals and teachers' performance were up for discussion, surface compliance could give way to an active search for performance shortcomings that lie within the responsibility of the school, capacity deficits that demand state and district action, and solutions that are consistently evaluated. Considering many teachers' unawareness, this process of internal accountability would have to be a schoolwide process in which administrators and higher-performing colleagues formulate expectations, set reachable standards, and impart skills and motivation to lower-performing colleagues.

Probation did not trigger such a process or seemed even to have preempted it. The school improvement plans written in the two states according to state-provided templates are a good indicator of this insufficiently internalized approach to school accountability. The plans, helpful as they were as organizing devices in the internal management and in the external monitoring of some schools, were neither strategic nor fine-grained enough to guide an internal accountability process. If they were strategic, they would have abstained from undue comprehensiveness. Instead, they would highlight the schools' main problems that were internally controllable and prioritize the main steps the school could have taken in a given year. If they were fine-grained, they would spell out a process of internal inquiry into classroom instruction and bridge between present instructional performance and ambitious goals. Such a fine-grained approach is necessary in accountability systems that press teachers to change their pedagogy, as both the Maryland and Kentucky assessments aim to do. In such systems, "alignment" entails a more complex process that moves beyond a concern for coverage, frequency of activities, and discrete skills learned in staff development workshops.

IMPROVING PROBATION POLICIES

How could probation policies be improved? One way might be raising the stakes—tightening the pressure. This, one could argue, might make higher test scores a more compelling goal for teachers. Others have argued that investment in capacity is germane, pointing to glaring deficits in schools serving the urban and rural poor. Finally, one could search for ways to make the accountability system more meaningful so that teachers would connect it more readily to their own work. It seems that regardless of the specific form a low-performing school's program might take, such programs need to tackle instructional skills and organizational effectiveness as well as educators' professional norms of performance and commitment to stay in the low-performing school.

Pressure

Some external pressure seems to be needed, but it should be mild. On one hand, teachers in the 11 schools on probation showed a conspicuous disinclination to assess themselves critically, so a signal expressing the concern of a supervising agency about a school's low performance seems to be necessary to lend legitimacy to the more proactive parts of a faculty. But on the other hand, too much pressure might sap teachers' commitment to the stigmatized school. After all, teachers have two options for escaping probation: They can strive for increased test scores, so that their school can exit probation, or they can exit the school. And exit they did. In the more urban Maryland schools, teacher turnover reached a level at which it is no longer possible to argue that the "right" teachers—that is, those who are presumably less willing to work hard—were leaving.

Many teachers and teacher leaders remained active and committed not because they expected rewards or felt that probation was good pressure but because they felt a more diffuse attachment to students and adults at their sites. They did not want "to let their school down," regardless of the school's prospects. These diffuse commitments were the undercurrents beneath the accountability system's rationalist incentive structure. Schools benefited from these moral commitments. It is quite likely that a rapid drain of more qualified teachers or teacher leaders—a widely feared negative consequence of probation—might not have happened in the 11 schools exactly because probation pressures had heretofore been rather benign.

But this could change if increased pressure foisted upon teachers a more straightforward calculation with rewards, costs, and benefits. Then forgone rewards and satisfactions due to probation pressures would become more accentuated and would be weighed against teachers' skepticism about accountability, dim expectations of success, and dissatisfaction with difficult work conditions. On the organizational level, more pressure might encourage more organizational rigidity and forestall the kinds of organizational learning processes that are necessary for more complex pedagogy to take root.

Therefore, making probation more forceful by raising the stakes and increasing pressure without making it more compelling for teachers to work in the negatively labeled schools does not seem a promising strategy. Instead, policies are needed that bring the problem of teacher retention and organizational stability centrally into focus. Here high-stakes accountability systems, including the recent federal Title I accountability regime, have been mostly silent.

Capacity

Investment in school capacity is key for the success of probation policies. In our schools, level of school capacity is the factor that best explains individual and organizational responses to probation. Work motivation and commitment to stay were strongly related to principal leadership, collegiality, and perceived skills of colleagues. We found these skills and talents in short supply across the studied schools. Of the many principals and instructional specialists we encountered, only a few were able to at least help their school to reach the "low-hanging fruit." Many more faltered, and when skillful leaders left their schools, gains were immediately in jeopardy because equally skillful people were not readily available to replace them. Thus, a broad-based strategy of enhancing the overall capacity of educators in the whole system is needed to increase the likelihood that more and more schools can be staffed with teachers who can teach effective lessons at least on a basic level and with administrators who have at least minimum competencies to run an organization effectively. Implementing the ambitious pedagogical aims of the two accountability systems would increase the need for capacity building for all teachers many times over.

Meaning

Contrary to assurances by policymakers and high-level administrators that their accountability system is fair, this was not a widely shared belief among teachers in the 11 schools, many of whom struggled with extraordinarily difficult circumstances. The fact that these sentiments were strong and consistent across two states with somewhat different accountability system designs speaks to ingrained cultural beliefs and attitudes among teachers who resist these systems as presently constructed. Accountability designs need to be adjusted so that more teachers in these schools feel evaluated fairly. To avoid unproductive blame shifting, accountability needs to be constructed as a multilateral system of shared responsibility among all participants in the educational process. Such a system would enable educators to carefully distinguish between barriers of performance that are caused externally and internally and then take full responsibility for the latter. Reviews or inspections conducted by trained personnel, sophisticated enough to tease out schools' contribution and improvement potential, are crucial in this endeavor.

Assessments and performance indicators that educators can embrace as valid make the connection between external expectations and teachers' own performance. Only in this way would the accountability system take on a normative power in shaping teacher expectations and conduct. Merely setting high expectations and engaging in tough talk will not be successful unless ways can be found to facilitate internalization of indicators as criteria for self-evaluation. This is paramount if the intention is to effect educational change beyond compliance with a simple and unambitious test for which a strategy of managerial and instructional control may be sufficient.

One way of facilitating internalization is giving schools the option to chose from a range of indicators that make sense to them, given the school's student population and the level of proficiency. This range of indicators should more adequately mirror the complexity of a school's educational tasks. Basic skills, higher-order thinking, citizenship, and the school's care for the well-being and positive stimulation of its students should be measured. Schools would establish baselines on the selected indicators for which they would then be held to continuous improvement. The California accountability system for alternative schools, for example, is attempting to do just that. A system like this could be expanded to regular schools. School-selected indicators could be used side by side with a statewide academic skills test. But high stakes would be attached to school-selected indicators as well.

A repertoire of indicators together with a review system that helps schools discern internally caused performance barriers and identify state and district responsibilities would then be the basis for a holistic decision about a school's performance status. When educators from the 11 schools were asked on the survey about their suggestions for improving the accountability system, the most popular suggestion was for external professionals knowledgeable about the school to evaluate teacher performance.

The story of the Maryland and Kentucky cases has shown that the language of sanctions will in all likelihood not become acceptable and fruitful without accompanying strategies of capacity building. But beyond that, accountability designs need to evolve into systems that can be embraced as valid, fair, and realistic by those who work under challenging conditions and find themselves, hopefully temporarily, on the losing side. Accountability systems that challenge teachers not only to intensify instruction but also to expand their pedagogical repertoires are particularly in need of a meaningful connection between external expectations and the teacher as learner.

CRAFTING A PROACTIVE RESPONSE AT SCHOOL

At the school level, whether principals adopted an outright control strategy, failed to exert any control, used more indirect means of control through programmatic standardization and mandated instructional surface structures, or inundated teachers with professional development and new programs, these strategies were accompanied in most cases by an absence of dialogue on professional norms and with inattention to teachers' commitment. This is understandable in light of the fact that, for many of the schools, new pressures, external micromanagement, and programmatic mandates had in fact constrained the school's space to craft its own strategy and that high teacher turnover, particularly in the Maryland schools, made continuous improvement difficult and work on school culture less promising.

But data from these schools, whether moving or stuck, suggest that schools facing sanctions and the label of low performance cannot circumvent the dialogue about their own shortcomings as much as the shortcomings of the accountability system. They cannot circumvent working on feelings of resentment, unfair treatment, self-worth, and responsibility. And they need to deliberate their educational ideals in light of student performance, accountability goals, and performance measures. Without such dialogue, instructional reform cannot become deep enough to move beyond training in surface activities and schools cannot overcome the problem of teacher motivation and retention that beset even the more successful cases.

When accountability systems subject low-performing schools to an audit, encourage them to analyze data and make data-driven decisions, compel them to accept accountability goals as givens, mandate them to compile a school improvement plan and expect them to monitor its implementation, they tend to favor the technical side of school improvement. For many schools, these steps alone pose serious challenges. It is nevertheless essential for school leaders to create space for the cultural and relational aspects of the improvement process and resist the defaults of increasing control and proliferating programs that hold the false promise of a swift and determined response to high stakes. A good start may be to insist on asking which aspects of accountability and probation represent good pressure and which ones are bad for the school, given educators' ideals, students' needs, and schools' share of responsibility for the problems at hand.

Accountability systems are rarely the result of experts designing the best possible system. They are political compromises. As such, they need to evolve. They must be improved at the state level and critically appropriated at the school level. This book attempted to show what could be done.

Appendix

Table A.1. The Seven Maryland Schools

	School Type	Enrollment (Sept. 1999)	Location	Percent Eligible for Free or Reduced-Price Lunch	Duration on Probation in 1998
School A	Middle	796	District B Inner suburban ring	50%	Just identified
School B	Middle	631	District B Inner suburban ring	40%	Just identified
School C	Elementary	498	District B Inner suburban ring	65%	Just identified
School D	Middle	1,222	District A Inner city	70%	3 years
School E	Elementary	388	District A Inner city	90%	3 years
School F	Elementary	409	District A Inner city	80%	Just identified
School G	Middle	633	District A City's edge	40–60%	Just identified

Table A.2. The Four Kentucky Schools

	School Type	Enrollment	Location	Percent Eligible for Free or Reduced-Price Lunch	Proportion of Minority Students	Duration on Probation
School 10	Elementary	460	Small town	92%	10%	2 biennia
School 20	Middle	760	City	42%	36%	1 biennium
School 30	Elementary	580	Small town	82%	46%	1 biennium
School 40	Middle	900	Large city	80%	47%	2 biennia

Table A.3. Teacher Survey

	Maryland	Kentucky
African American	77%	11%
Female	79%	84%
Average age	39	42.5
Response rate	58%	47%

Note: We relied on our own interview material for items that related to accountability and probation. We also consulted the work by Kelley and Protsik (1997) on teacher motivation, by LeCompte and Dworkin (1991) on burnout, by Ashton and Webb (1986) on teacher efficacy, and by McLaughlin and Talbert (1993) on school culture. Our analysis is based on a total of 250 interviews, 267 survey respondents, and 70 classroom observations. Further details can be retrieved from the technical report at: *www.gseis.ucla.edu/faculty/mintrop/Schools-on-probation/schools-on-probation-cover-overall.htm*

Table A.4. Scales Constructed from the Teacher Survey

Scale Item	Factor Loading
Goal Importance	
• It really does not make much difference to me whether this school gets off the reconstitution-eligibility list/the list of schools eligible for a highly skilled educator. (Values are reversed.)	−.698
• It is very important for me personally that the school raise performance scores.	.627
• A high score on the MSPAP means a lot to me./Achievement rewards on the state accountability system (KIRIS/CATS) mean a lot to me.	.634
• It says nothing about me personally as a teacher whether the school raises its performance score or not. (Values are reversed.)	−.507

Reliability (Cronbach alpha) = .72

Scale Item	Factor Loading
Validity of Assessment	
• The MSPAP/the state assessment (KIRIS/CATS) assesses all the things I find important for students to learn.	.742
• A good teacher has nothing to fear from the MSPAP / the state accountability system (KIRIS/CATS).	.548
• The MSPAP/the state assessment (KIRIS/CATS) reflects just plain good teaching.	.727

Reliability (Cronbach alpha) = .75

Scale Item	Factor Loading
(Un)fairness	
• For the most part, teachers are unfairly judged by the accountability system.	.506
• I resent being judged based on the performance of other teachers on the basis of schoolwide test scores.	.610
• The accountability system is stacked against schools located in poor communities.	.704
• I feel that I am working to my best ability and effort despite the low scores the school received.	.600
• If somebody from the state or district thinks they can do a better job than teachers here, let them take over.	.504

Reliability (Cronbach alpha) = .77

(continued)

Table A.4. (*continued*)

Scale Item	Factor Loading
(Un)realism	
• Our students are not behind because of the teachers they have but because of the conditions in which they have to grow up.	.638
• The performance expectations of the state are for the most part unrealistic.	.638
• It is unrealistic to expect schools that serve poor neighborhoods to perform on the same level as schools in wealthy neighborhoods.	.634
• The MSPAP / the state assessment (KIRIS/CATS) is unrealistic because too many tasks are too hard for our students.	.543
Reliability (Cronbach alpha) = .73	
Direction	
• The accountability goals provide a focus for my teaching efforts.	—
• Accountability goals tell us what is important for the school to accomplish.	—
• Prior to actual testing, benchmarks and public release items gave me a pretty good idea of the content of the MSPAP / the state assessments (KIRIS/CATS).	—
• I am not sure exactly what our students are expected to do on the MSPAP / the state assessments (KIRIS/CATS). (Values are reversed.)	—
Reliability (Cronbach alpha) = .60	
Efficacy	
• If I try really hard, I can get through to even the most difficult or unmotivated student.	.693
• By trying a different teaching method, I can significantly affect a student's achievement.	.630
• There is really very little I can do to ensure that most of my students achieve at a high level. (Values are reversed.)	−.622
• Many of the students I teach are not capable of learning the material I should be teaching them. (Values are reversed.)	−.540
Reliability (Cronbach alpha) = .71	
Professionalism	
My colleagues would see me as:	
• A leader	.620
• Very knowledgeable	.625
• Enthusiastic	.591
• Effective	.576
• Highly educated	.554
• Exceptional	.537
• Very professional	.553
Reliability (Cronbach alpha) = .79	

(*continued*)

Table A.4. (*continued*)

Scale Item	*Factor Loading*
Personal Skills	
• I believe that I have the skills and knowledge needed for our school to meet the performance expectations of the state.	—
• I know how to teach so that students do well on the MSPAP/KIRIS/CATS.	—
Collegiality	
• Most of my colleagues share my beliefs and values about what the central mission of the school should be.	.597
• There is a great deal of cooperative effort among staff here.	.874
• I can count on colleagues here when I feel down about my teaching or my students.	.809
• In this school, the faculty discusses major decisions and sees to it that they are carried out.	.678
Reliability (Cronbach alpha) = .83	
Principal Support	
• The school administration's behavior toward the staff is supportive and encouraging.	.739
• The principal usually consults with staff members before he/she makes decisions that affect teachers.	.884
• Staff members are recognized for a job well done.	.605
Reliability (Cronbach alpha) = .78	
Principal Control	
• The principal sets priorities, makes plans, and sees that they are carried out.	.595
• The principal puts pressure on teachers to get results.	.615
• In this school, the principal tells us what the district and the state expect of us, and we comply.	.534
Reliability (Cronbach alpha) = .67	
Colleagues' Skills	
• My teaching colleagues have the knowledge and skills needed for our school to meet the performance expectations of the state.	—
• The typical teacher at this school ranks near the top of the teaching profession in knowledge and skills.	—

Extraction method: Principal Axis Factoring.

Rotation method: Oblimin with Kaiser Normalization.

References

Abelmann, C., Elmore, R., Even, J., Kenyon, S., & Marshall, J. (1999). *When accountability knocks, will anyone answer?* (CPRE Research Report Series RR-42). Philadelphia: Consortium for Policy Research in Education.

Ashton, P., & Webb, R. B. (1986). *Making a difference: Teachers' sense of efficacy and student achievement.* New York: Longman.

Bennett, C., & Ferlie, E. (1994). *Managing crisis and change in health care: The organizational response to HIV/AIDS.* Philadelphia: Open University Press.

Blair, J. (2000, August 2). Districts wooing teachers with bonuses, incentives. *Education Week on the Web* [Online]. Available: www. edweek.org/

Boser, U. (2001, January 11). Pressure without support. *Education Week,* pp. 68–71.

Brady, R. (2003). *Can failing schools be fixed?* Washington, DC: Thomas B. Fordham Foundation.

Chicago Public Schools. (1997). *School probation information packet.* Chicago: Office of Accountability.

Cibulka, J., & Lindle, J. (2001). *The politics of accountability for school improvement in Kentucky and Maryland* (Technical Report). Washington, DC: Office of Educational Research and Improvement, U.S. Department of Education.

Cohen, D. K. (1990). A revolution in one classroom: The case of Mrs. Oublier. *Educational Evaluation & Policy Analysis, 12,* 311–329.

Cohen, D. K., & Ball, D. L. (1999). *Instruction, capacity and improvement* (CPRE Research Report Series, RP-42). Consortium for Policy Research in Education. University of Pennsylvania.

Cohen, D. K., McLaughlin, M. W., & Talbert, J. E. (1993). *Teaching for understanding: Challenges for policy and practice.* San Francisco: Jossey-Bass.

Cuban, L. (1984). *How teachers taught: Constancy and change in American classrooms 1890–1980.* New York: Longman.

Darling-Hammond, L. (1991). The implications of testing policy for quality and equality. *Phi Delta Kappan, 73,* 220–225.

Darling-Hammond, L. (1997). School reform at the crossroads: Confronting the central issues of teaching. *Educational Policy, 11*(2), 151–166.

Darling-Hammond, L., & Wise, A. E. (1985). Beyond standardization: State standards and school improvement. *The Elementary School Journal, 85*(3), 315–336.

David, J., Kannapel, P., & McDiarmid., C. (2000). *The influence of distinguished educators on school improvement: A study of Kentucky's school intervention program.* Lexington, KY: Partnership for Kentucky Schools.

Dworkin, A. G. (1987). *Teacher burnout in the public schools: Structural causes and consequences for children*. Albany: State University of New York Press.

Elmore, R. F. (1990). *Restructuring schools: The next generation of educational reform*. San Francisco: Jossey-Bass.

Finkelstein, B., Malen, B., Muncey, D., Rice, J., Croninger, R., Briggs, L., Redmond Jones, D., & Thrasher, K. (2000). *Mired in contradictions: The first two years of a reconstitution initiative*. College Park: University of Maryland.

Firestone, W. (1996). Images of teaching and proposals for reform: A comparison of ideas from cognitive and organizational research. *Educational Administration Quarterly, 32*(2), 209–235.

Firestone, W. A., Mayrowetz, D., & Fairman, J. (1998). Performance-based assessment and instructional change: The effects of testing in Maine and Maryland. *Educational Evaluation and Policy Analysis, 20*(2), 95–113.

Firestone, W., & Pennell, J. (1993). Teacher commitment, working conditions, and differential incentive policies. *Review of Educational Research, 63*(4), 489–525.

Fuhrman, S., & Elmore, R. (2001). Holding schools accountable: Is it working? *Phi Delta Kappan, 83*(1), 67–72.

Fuhrman, S., & Odden, A. R. (2001). Introduction: A Kappan special section on school reform. *Phi Delta Kappan, 83*(1), 59–61.

Goals 2000: Educate America Act. (1994). H.R. 1804, 102nd Cong., 2d Sess.

Grant, S.G. (1998). *Reforming reading, writing and mathematics: Teachers' responses and the prospects for systemic reform*. Mahwah, NJ: Erlbaum.

Gray, J. (2000). *Causing concern but improving: A review of schools' experiences* (Research Report No. 188). Norwich, England: Department for Education and Employment.

Hanushek, E. A. (1994). *Making schools work: Improving performance and controlling costs*. Washington, DC: Brookings Institution Press.

Hargreaves, A. (1994). *Changing teachers, changing times: Teachers' work and culture in the postmodern age*. New York: Teachers College Press.

Hargreaves, A. & Fullan, M. (Eds.). (1992). *Understanding teacher development*. New York: Teachers College Press.

Hess, G. A., Jr. (1999a). Expectations, opportunity, capacity, and will: The four essential components of Chicago school reform. *Educational Policy, 13*(4), 494–517.

Hess, G. A., Jr. (1999b). Understanding achievement (and other) changes under Chicago school reform. *Educational Evaluation and Policy Analysis, 21*(1), 67–83.

Ingersoll, R. (2001). Teacher turnover and teacher shortages: An organizational analysis. *American Educational Research Journal, 38*(3), 499–534.

Johnson, S. M. (1990). *Teachers at work: Achieving success in our schools*. New York: Basic Books.

Johnston, R. (2000, February 22). *Troubled PA districts eye dramatic changes* [Online]. Available: www.edweek.com/ewstory.cfm?slug=12pah20

Jones, R. (1997, February 19). Teachers head to court, students hit streets to protest school plan. *Philadelphia Inquirer*, p. B-1.

Kelley, C. (1999). The motivational impact of school-based performance awards. *Journal of Personnel Evaluation in Education, 12*(4), 309–326.

Kelley, C., Conley, S., & Kimball, S. (2000). Payment for results: Effects of the Kentucky and Maryland group-based performance award programs. *Peabody Journal of Education, 75*(4), 159–199.

Kelley, C., & Protsik, J. (1997). Risk and reward: Perspectives on the implementation of Kentucky's school-based performance award program. *Educational Administration Quarterly, 33*, 474–505.

Knapp, M. S. (1997). Between systemic reforms and the mathematics and science classroom: The dynamics of innovation, implementation, and professional learning. *Review of Educational Research, 67*, 227–266.

Lawler, E. (1973). *Motivation in work organizations.* San Francisco: Jossey-Bass.

LeCompte, M., & Dworkin, A. (1991). *Giving up on school: Student drop-outs and teacher burn-outs.* Newbury Park, CA.: Corwin.

Levine, C., Rubin, I., & Wolohojian, G. (1982). Managing organizational retrenchment: Preconditions, deficiencies, and adaptations in the public sector. *Administration and Society, 14*(1), 101–136.

Louis, K. S., & Kruse, S. (1998). Creating community in reform: Images of organizational learning in inner-city schools. In K. Leithwood & K. Seashore Louis (Eds.), *Organizational learning in schools* (pp. 17–46). Lisse, Netherlands: Swets & Zeitlinger.

Malen, B. (1999). On rewards, punishments and possibilities: Teacher compensation as an instrument for education reform. *Journal of Personnel Evaluation in Education, 12*(4), 387–394.

Malen, B., Croninger, R., Muncey, D., & Redmond-Jones, D. (2002). Reconstituting schools: "Testing" the "theory of action." *Educational Evaluation and Policy Analysis, 24*(2), 113–132.

Maryland State Department of Education. (1997). *Criteria for reconstitution.* Baltimore: Author.

McLaughlin, M. W., & Talbert, J. E. (1993). *Contexts that matter for teaching and learning: Strategic opportunities for meeting the nation's educational goals.* Stamford, CT: Center for Research on the Context of Secondary School Teaching.

McNeil, L. M. (2000). *Contradictions of school reform: Educational costs of standardized testing.* New York: Routledge.

Mintrop, H. (1999). Changing core beliefs and practices through systemic reform: The case of Germany after the fall of socialism. *Educational Evaluation and Policy Analysis, 31*(3), 271–296.

Mintrop, H. (2003). The limits of sanctions in low-performing schools. *Educational Policy Analysis Archives* [Online], *11*(3). Available: http://epaa.asu.edu/epaa/v11n3.html

Mintrop, H., & MacLellan, A. (2002). School improvement plans in elementary and middle schools on probation. *The Elementary School Journal, 102*(4), 275–300.

Mintrop, H., MacLellan, A., & Quintero, M. (2001). School improvement plans in schools on probation: A comparative content analysis across three accountability systems. *Educational Administration Quarterly, 37*(2), 197–218.

Mohrman, A. M., Jr. , Mohrman, S. A., & Odden, A. R. (1996). Aligning teacher compensation with systemic school reform: Skill-based pay and group-based performance rewards. *Educational Evaluation and Policy Analysis, 18*(1), 51–71.

National Commission on Excellence in Education. (1983). A nation at risk: The imperative for educational reform: Text of the report. *The Chronicle of Higher Education, 26*, 11–16.

Newmann, F. M., King, M. B., & Rigdon, M. (1997). Accountability and school performance: Implications from restructuring schools. *Harvard Educational Review, 67*(1), 41–74.

Noble, A. J., & Smith, M. L. (1994). Old and new beliefs about measurement-driven reform: "Build it and they will come." *Educational Policy, 8*(2), 111–136.

O'Day, J. (2003). Complexity, accountability, and school improvement. In S. Fuhrman & R. Elmore (Eds.), *Redesigning accountability systems*. New York: Teachers College Press.

O'Day, J. A., Goertz, M. E., & Floden, R. E. (1995). *Building capacity for education reform*. New Brunswick, NJ: Consortium for Policy Research in Education, U.S. Department of Education, Office of Educational Research and Improvement, Educational Resources Information Center.

O'Day, J. A., & Smith, M. S. (1993). Systemic reform and educational opportunity. In S. H. Fuhrman (Ed.), *Designing coherent education policy: Improving the system* (pp. 250–312). San Francisco: Jossey-Bass.

Odden, A., & Kelley, C. (1997). *Paying teachers for what they know and do: New and smarter compensation strategies to improve schools*. Thousand Oaks, CA: Corwin Press.

Pankratz, R. S., & Petrosko, J. M. (Eds.). (2000). *All children can learn: Lessons from the Kentucky reform experience*. San Francisco: Jossey-Bass.

Peterson, P., Rabe, B., & Wong, K. (1991). The maturation of redistributive programs. In A. Odden (Ed.), *Education policy implementation* (pp. 65–80). Albany: State University of New York Press.

Price, H. (1997, February). *"No excuses" era of urban school reform*. Keynote address delivered at The Urban League, New York.

Quality counts 2001: A better balance. (2001). *Education Week, 20*(17), 8–193.

Riley, R. W. (1997, February 18). *Putting standards of excellence in action*. Fourth Annual State of American Education Address, The Carter Center, Atlanta, GA. Available online: www.ed.gov/speeches/02-1997

Rosenholtz, S. (1991). *Teachers' work place: The social organization of schools*. New York: Teachers College Press.

Rowan, B., Chiang, F. S., & Miller, R. J. (1997). Using research on employees' performance to study the effects of teachers on student's achievement. *Sociology of Education, 70*(4), 256–284.

Ruenzel, D. (1997). Do or die. *Teacher Magazine, 8*, 24–30.

Schein, E. (1991). *Organizational culture and leadership*. San Francisco: Jossey-Bass.

Schemo, D. (2002, August 28). Few exercise new right to leave failing schools. *New York Times,* pp. 1, 14.

Senge, P. M. (1990). *The fifth discipline: The art and practice of the* nization. New York: Doubleday.

Shamir, B. (1991). Meaning, self, and motivation in organizations. *Studies, 12*(3), 405–424.

Shulman, L. (1987). Knowledge and teaching: Foundations for the *Harvard Educational Review, 57*(1), 1–22.

Spillane, J. P., & Jennings, N. E. (1997). Aligned instructional policy pedagogy: Exploring instructional reform form the classroom *Teachers College Record, 98*(3), 449–481.

Staw, B. M., Lance, E., & Dutton, J. (1981). Threat-rigidity effects in c behavior: A multilevel analysis. *Administrative Science Quarterly,*

Stecher, B., Barron, S., Chun, T., & Ross, K. (2000). *The effects of the State education reform on schools and classrooms* (CSE Technical Los Angeles: CRESST.

Stoll, L., & Myers, K. (Eds.). (1998). *No quick fixes: Perspectives o difficulty.* London: Falmer Press.

Thompson, C., & Zeuli, J. (1999). The frame and the tapestry: Stan reform and professional development. In L. Darling-Hammond (Eds.), *Teaching as the learning profession: Handbook of policy* (pp. 341–375). San Francisco: Jossey-Bass.

Vroom, V. H. (1964). *Work and motivation.* New York: Wiley.

Wilcox, B., & Gray, J. (1996). *Inspecting schools: Holding schools to a helping schools to improve.* Buckingham, England: Open Univers

Whitford, B. L. (Ed.). (2000). *Accountability, assessment, and teacher c Lessons from Kentucky's reform efforts.* Albany: State University of Press.

Wong, K. K., Anagnostopoulos, D., & Rutledge, S. (1998, November). *dation and conflict: The implementation of Chicago's probation an tution policies.* Paper presented at the annual meeting of the Asso Public Policy Analysis and Management, New York.

Wong, K. K., Anagnostopoulos, D., Rutledge, S., Lynn, L., & Dreeben, *Implementation of an educational accountability agenda: Integrated g in the Chicago public schools enters its fourth year.* Chicago: Uni Chicago, Department of Education.

Index

About the Author

AFTER HAVING BEEN A TEACHER in the United States and Germany, Heinrich Mintrop is now an associate professor at the University of California, Los Angeles. His interest is the study of large-scale educational policies and change in schools and classrooms. He co-authored a book on educational change and social transformation in Germany after the fall of the Berlin Wall. In recent years, he has published on issues of accountability, democracy, and constructivism in American schools and cross-nationally. At UCLA, he is on the leadership team of the Principal Leadership Institute, which focuses on the improvement of urban schools.